FIGURE DRAWING

Made easy for beginners

Detailed step by step art tutorial book

DR. MANJUNATH V RAO (M.B.B.S)

To my Grandparents, Mom, Dad and Brother.

Thanks to all my friends who inspired me, supported me and encouraged me.

Special Thanks to Dr.Shivaprasad Hiremath, Dr.Rishab Mahale, Dr.Shashank N, K Siddartha D Shetty, Dr.Adithya R S, Dr.Shashank K Gowda, Dr.Sharath M, Dr.Yatish Gujjar, Harish, Hemanth, Shashank A, Naveen, Adarsha, Sachin, Monish, Dr.Ravitheja, Dr.Eshan, Dr.Ashish, Pooja R, Sachin R, Dr.Hruday, Dr.Saiprasad, Dr.Prajwal Patil, Dr.Sujith Kulkarni, Dr.Revanth, Dr.Toran Prakash, Dr.Surya S R L, Poojith, Vinod, Yashwanth, Shailender, Sujith, Prabhu, Pradeep Anna who have helped me in various way when it came to influencing me, suggesting changes, giving new ideas, acting as critics and helping me in creating this book.

And also thanks to my publishers and their support without which this could not have been possible.

Preface

Beginner word itself has the word "begin" in it.

Beginning is the 1st step of my Instruction and the most important step. With that LETS SET GO...!!!!!!
So now that you have accepted the fact that you are beginner and about to begin, most important thing is that you should never judge yourself and your work until you reach minimum of 9 months of practice. This applies same to not giving damn about others opinion till minimum of 9 months....

Next step is consistent daily effort, repetitive daily actions directed towards your goal is very important. Even if you feel no improvement or slightest of improvement, don't stop. Perseverance is very crucial to maintain your motive and remain as an artist.

Mere theory won't make you an artist, instead hold the pencil and start to scribble (FYI even scribbling is a form of art)

Then comes sticking on to your technique which you feel right. You can listen to others opinion but you never have to agree to what they say. Everyone has their own unique style and one has to stick to it without any doubt or second thought.

Lastly this book is designed specifically for absolute beginners focusing only on basic of getting basic outline right. ***I've not stressed about tone and values***. As a beginner you to learn the most important step i.e., to get proportion right. As you progress you'll get to know about light and values. So lets start with basic of getting outline right.

Once you start sketching, trust me, you'll loose track of time, you'll forget your worries, you'll forget your past & your future where in the present starts mattering to you the most and you will enter that zone where you get disconnected from the rest of the world.
Time will just drift away with each stroke of your pencil, lines will intersect, turn around and form beautiful pictures. The more you do it, the more confident you get and the more you enjoy. It will be just you, the pencil and the paper. Nothing else would matter.

And most importantly don't worry about the result. Who cares about what you have drawn, it is only you who should appreciate your work the most.
I'm saying this because this hindrance is a very big barrier to anyone when it comes to starting anything new. When we pay attention to what opinions others have, we loose the fun part of doing anything what we like to. Trust me, you are learning this for the sake of learning and not to impress others.
Once you have made your motive clear, we'll now begin to focus on the progress of our art journey.

Preface

Nothing miraculous will happen after you have finished taking glimpse of this book or reading it in detail. It's the consistent effort which you put on daily basis which matters the most. Few important starters when you start sketching should include the ones I've mentioned below.

SKETCH DAILY– biggest advice ever to get better at sketching one can receive.
OBSERVE– the key step in the process of sketching
EXPERIMENT– The best part about being a beginner is about experimenting and doing whatever & however you want
MAKE IT FUN– choose an ideal peaceful environment, add any music in the background and with a peace of mind begin sketching. This ain't assignment or exams to stress about.
EXPERIENCE THE JOY– whole purpose of being an artist. Don't do work under pressure and time constraints.
KEEP TRACK OF YOUR PROGRESS– keep looking back at old sketches, look for your mistakes, try not to repeat your mistake.
SHARE YOUR WORK WITH YOUR FRIENDS– Just the ones who are supportive to you and help you in a positive way.
DON'T CRITICISE YOUR WORK– Self criticism is very harmful for progression of your art journey, odd chances are that it might end your art journey.

There are many books which refer breaking sketch into 8 steps or 32 steps and so on. But I would say you can do sketching in only one step which would be put all your interest into it and do passionately.
I thank you audience for taking this step to go through an art journey of this book. I've given my best for you guys. I definitely hope you'll enjoy this book...

Contents

Preface   03

Introduction   06
The Basic step   07
Proportions of head   10
Measuring approximate proportions using pencil   11
Proportions of Human figure   12
Tone and Value   15
Male figure in standing   17
Male figure in sitting   30
Male figure in flexed posture   33
Male figure in action   38
Female Figure in standing   47
Female Figure in sitting   61
Female Figure in sleeping   73
Female Figure on couch   76
Female Figure in kneeling   77

Introduction

What is Art?
It is the expression or application of human creative skill and imagination, typically in a visual form Theories won't turn you into better artist and no one can turn you into a better artist unless you do it yourself.

Nude human figure study is most important part for any figure analysis and study. One should never be ashamed about the sight of body which we survive with. It is not at all feasible to draw clothed figure without the idea of form of figure and its structure. One cannot become a surgeon without knowledge of anatomy.

Artist will have to take 2 things into consideration
1. View point
2. Horizon

One has to address the height, width, proportions of a figure and consider all the elements without fail. All of us differ in appearance and construction.

Always be sure your art work answers these two question-
- What is Artists intention behind the drawing?
- What is Subjects expressions and feelings in the drawing?

Drawing equipments

Basic instruments
- Pencil - graphite pencils, charcoal pencil
- Eraser
- Pencil sharpener
- Ruler scale

Additional instrument
- Compass
- Stumps for blending
- French curves
- T square
- Paints
- Paint brushes
- Crayons

Make sure you have washed your hands properly or else might end up dirtying the paper with food stains from your hand. Keep above instruments in reach of your hand by placing a table next to where you sit and draw.

The Basic Step

The must learn most step when it comes to art learning-DRAW LINES FREE HANDEDLY

Make habit of drawing horizontal and vertical lines free handedly as much as possible especially if you are an absolute beginner

Most of us still require ruler scale for drawing a straight line.

Practice drawing straight lines as much as possible

Start practicing drawing circles and parallel lines free handedly

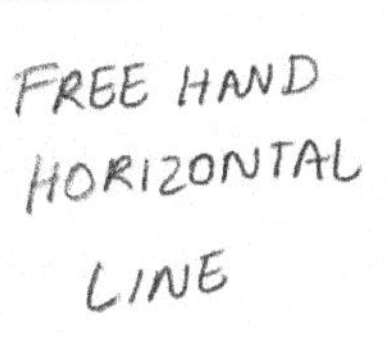

Once you get good at drawing straight lines and circles free hand-edly , it's time to upgrade your skill set.

Start practicing hatching, cross hatching, back and forth shading, stippling, scribbling and loose cir-cles.

Try to learn smudging. Try smudging with your finger.

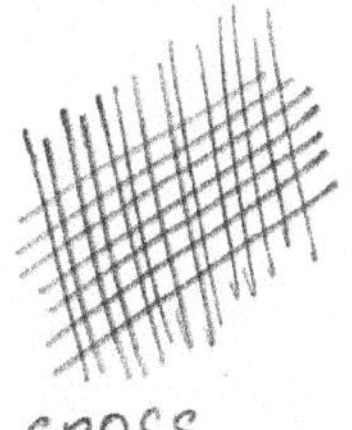

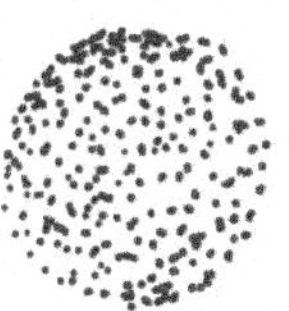

Practice Monitor

It is very important to track your progress on a daily basis. Below I've given a monitor chart so that you can track your routine. If you use up below chart, you can create your own chart. The numbers mentioned below indicates the dates of the month. The day you practice fill up the empty circle, if you haven't practiced one particular day, leave it blank. I definitely promise you if you stick on to the practice for at least 30 days in a row, you will improve to a great extent.

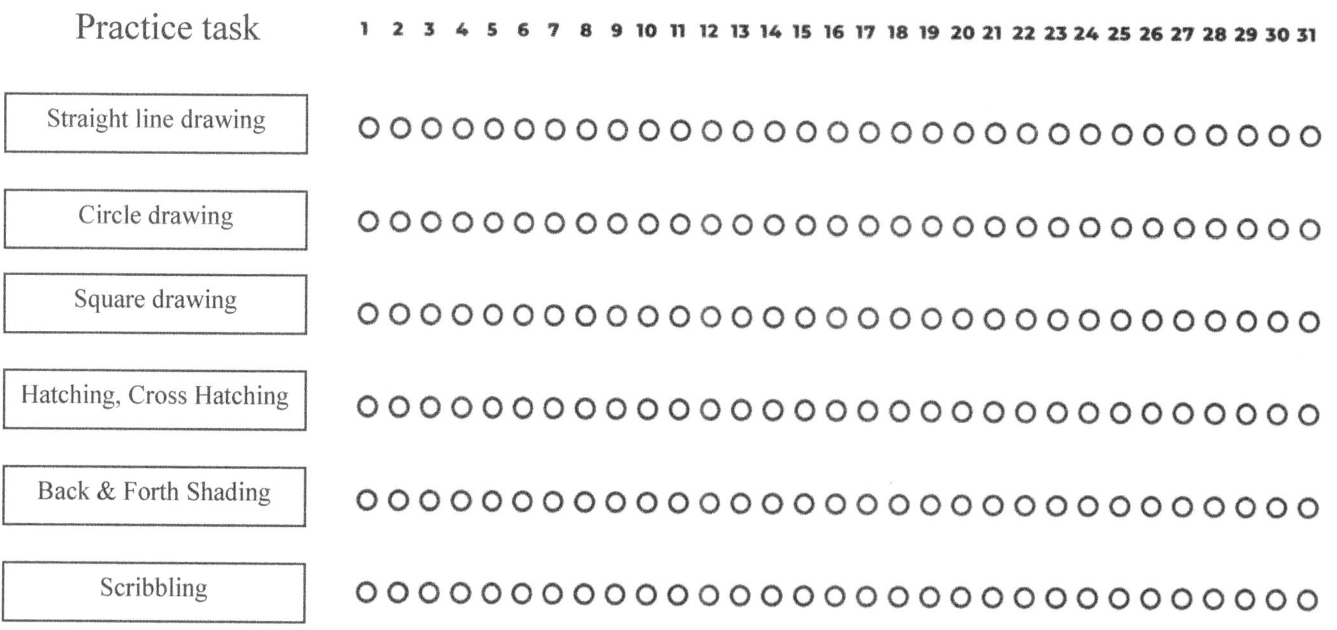

Practice task

Straight line drawing

Circle drawing

Square drawing

Hatching, Cross Hatching

Back & Forth Shading

Scribbling

Time table : Set up a schedule with time slot allotted in particular way that fits you. Example is given below.

From Date: 01-01-2022 To Date: 30-01-2022

Time	Activity
06:30 - 07:30	Art Practice
07:30 - 07:45	Break
07:45 - 08:30	Art Practice
09:00 - 16:00	Office Work hours
17:30 - 18:30	Art Practice
18:30 - 18:45	Break
18:45 - 19:30	Revisit Art made by you

Create a time table that you are comfortable with and one that suits you the best. I will assure you that you will be able to keep the track of your practice hours and will learn to efficiently in the process of understanding art.

"**Observation**" - the most important step

Observation is carefully examining and paying attention to the subject to capture its form accurately.

It involves analyzing
- Proportions
- Angles
- Structure
- How lights fall and shadows form
- Paying attention to the detail
- Breaking down the complex forms
- Constantly checking and comparing

Take your own time to understand the subject as this forms the basic ground for art work.

Better the observation, better the sketch you draw.

This is the most crucial step and you just need to pay full focus on the subject.

Look at the subject with focused attention, take as much as time possible.

Soon after observation, just start drawing, without overanalyzing. Jump into sketching part immediately, dive deep as you get along.

Work space: You can practice in space given below to draw the basics which you have learned here & see how much you've improved from before

Proportions of head

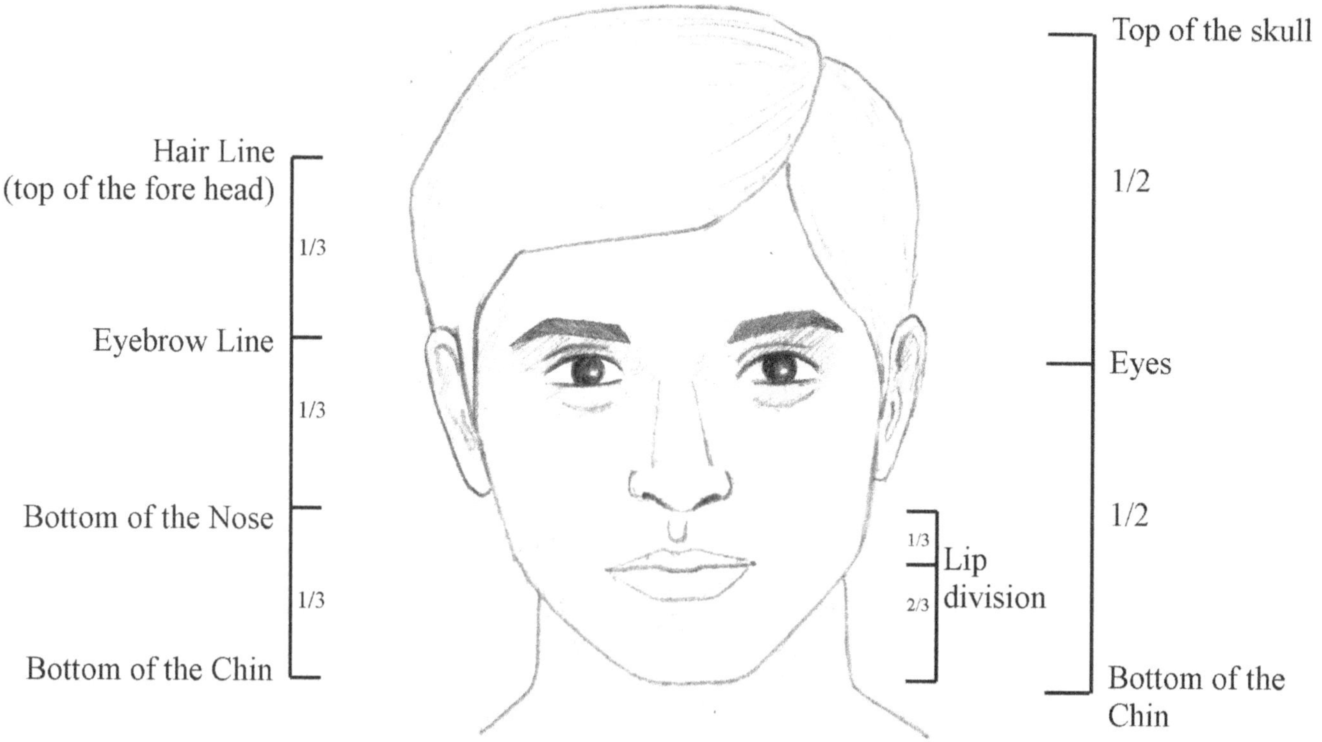

Hair Line (top of the fore head)

1/3

Eyebrow Line

1/3

Bottom of the Nose

1/3

Bottom of the Chin

Top of the skull

1/2

Eyes

1/2

Bottom of the Chin

1/3 2/3 Lip division

The very important element in the Portrait drawing is getting the facial proportion right. Even one disproportion can affect overall portrait to great extent. So before you begin sketching take as much time as you need to observe the facial proportion .

Hence 1st step for a properly proportioned portrait is to observe the model keenly with 100% concentration.

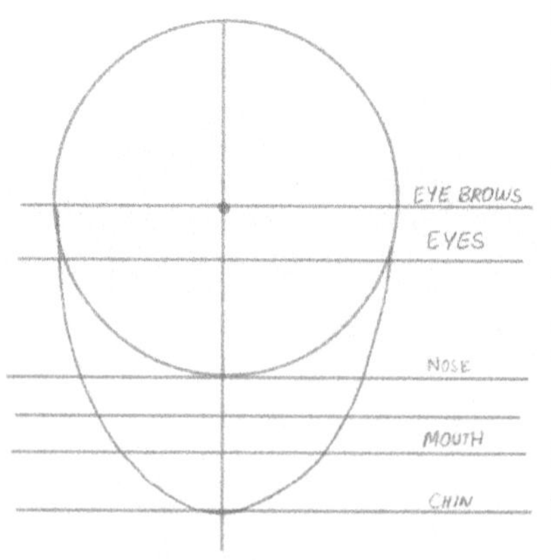

The Eyes are halfway between top of the head and chin
The Bottom of the nose is halfway between the eyes and chin
The Mouth is 1/3rd way between the nose and chin
Distance between the eyes is equal to the width of one eye

GOLDEN RATIO of the face = face is approximately 1.6 times longer than it is wide i.e.,   Length = 1.6 X Width

Measuring approximate proportions using pencil

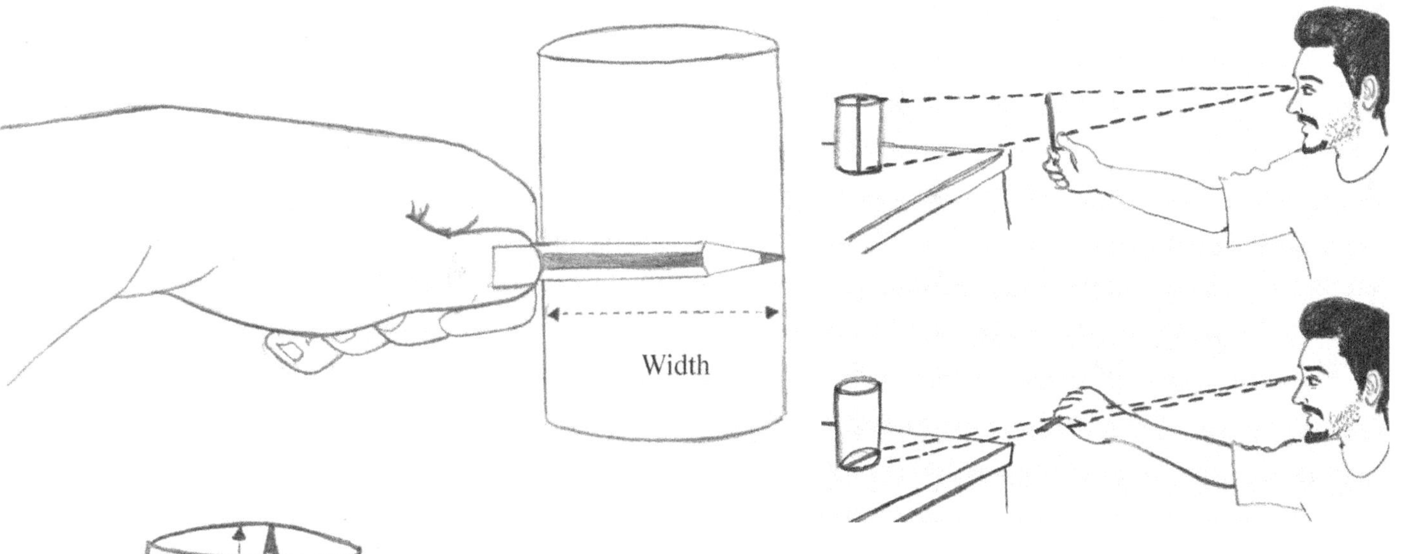

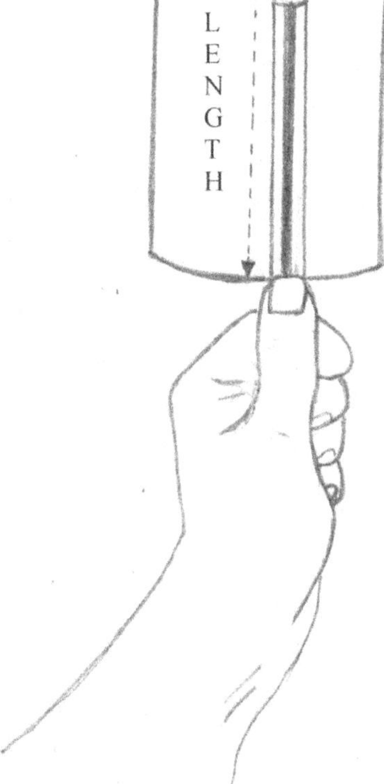

This is to get proportions right and it is very simple. All you need is to use pencil in hand to measure the length approximately.

Measure the length of the object horizontally or vertically by keeping pencil in front of object and keep your hand outstretched. The marking on your pencil shall guide you to get the dimensions right.

Now use this length on the pencil on the drawing sheet to get marvelous results in short time.

The pictures put here shows how to implement this method.

How to hold instruments

Typical position

For extremely free work

For work at comfort and ease

For detailed work

Proportions of Human Figure

Proportion measurement is of two type—Normal proportion
Ideal proportion

As a beginner,
- Average proportion should be taken
- Deviation from ideal proportion is fine
- Bit of variation here and there is fine

Proportion I have mentioned is of *Eight head proportion of Michelangelo* famous Italian artist from times of renaissance.

Other proportion includes seven and half head of Richter (famous French anatomist)

Precision of your art will depend on your observation.

More time you give and concentrate on model the better the outcome be.

Measuring proportion steps-
- Hold the pencil in the measuring hand
- Keep arms straight
- Do not vary distance between your hand & eye (if not you'll end up getting false size relationship)
- The top of the pencil should be at the top of models head
- Tip of your thumb at the chin of the model
- Using the exact length (Head length) now you can move your arm and measure anywhere
- This gives us the unit of measurement as *Head units*

Proportion of Human figure

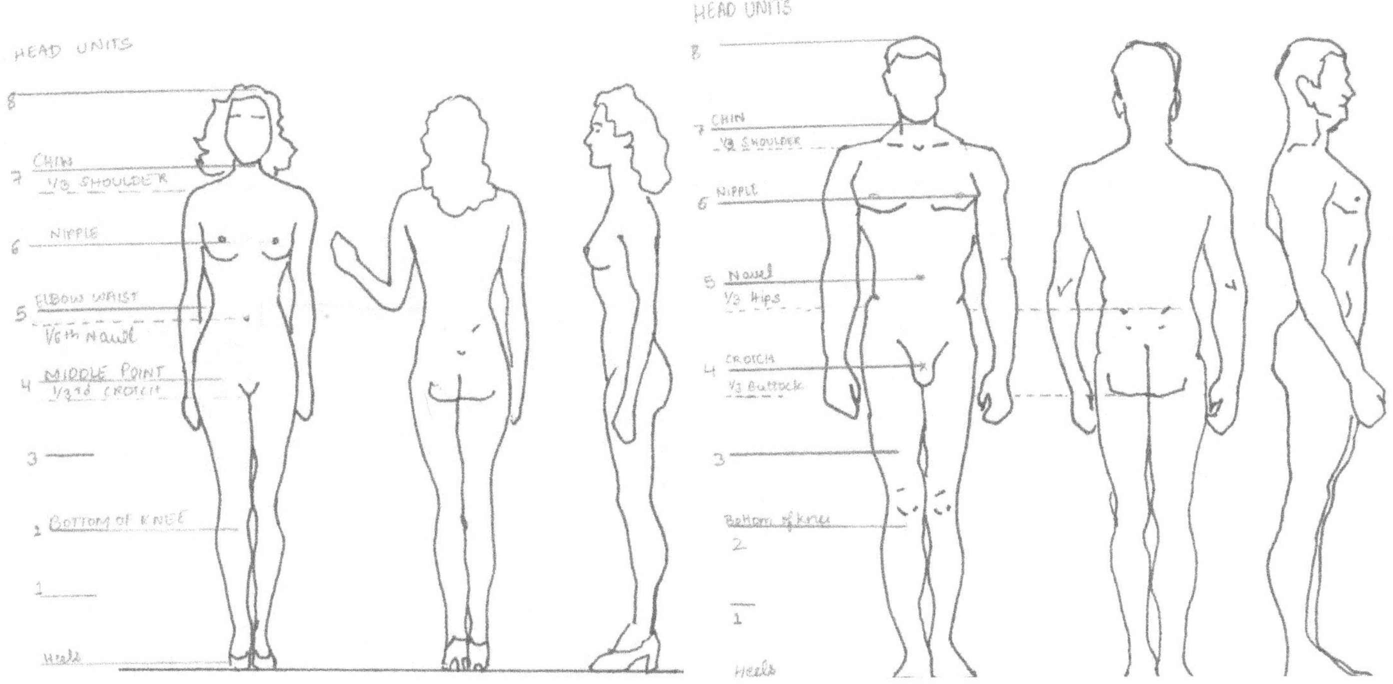

Proportion I have mentioned is of *Eight head proportion of Michelangelo* famous Italian artist from times of renaissance.

Height = 8 Head units
Width = 2.3 Head units

Notice various levels and their corresponding landmarks for finding easy way to learn proportions

Height = 8 Head units
Width = 2 Head units

Work space: You can practice in space given below to draw proportionate outlines of human figure which you have learned & see how much you've improved from before

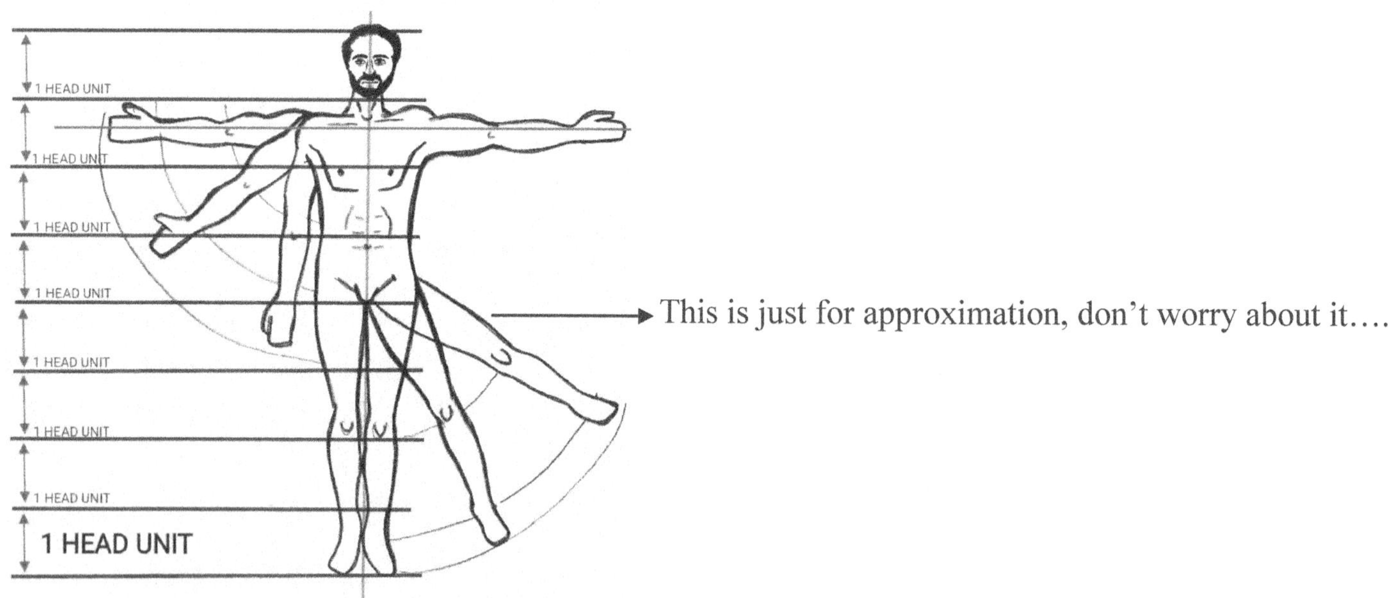

This is just for approximation, don't worry about it….

Tone and Value

Any object exposed to light has
- Light tone
- Middle tone
- Dark tone
- Reflected tone
- Shadows

This is what which gives 3 dimensional effect to the figure which we draw on a 2 dimensional plane paper

Notice the technique of how it works. Light falls on exposed part and leaves the shadow on the underneath parts. You can clearly make it out if you observe the face details and notice the shadows by yourself.

General rule:
Light falls on the forehead, nose, chins, cheeks, lips
Shadow is formed on the orbit, near nostril, underneath nose near nostril, underneath neck, underneath lip

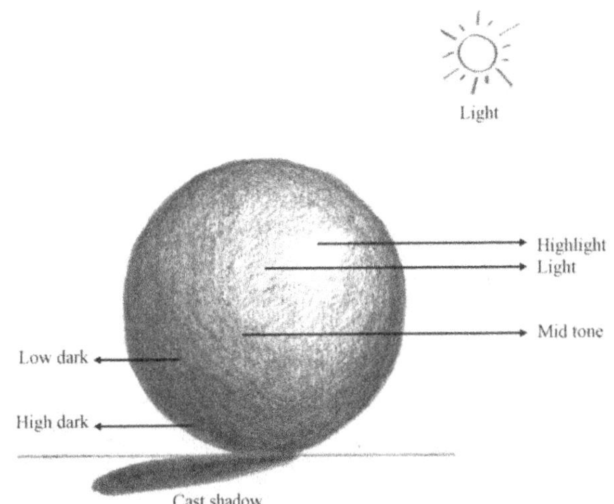

When it is not easy to understand figure from different position, we can use model like *Wooden Mannequin.*

It is practical to place the dummy in the same pose as model , turning it and drawing sketches from different point of view. This will be a good exercise for you as a beginner

There is no absolute formula to get proportions precisely right. Human error are bound to happen and I would consider it to be normal.

Most people say one cannot draw figures without the knowledge of anatomy, but that is a misunderstanding.
All the artists from before have done several masterpieces without great deal of anatomical knowledge.

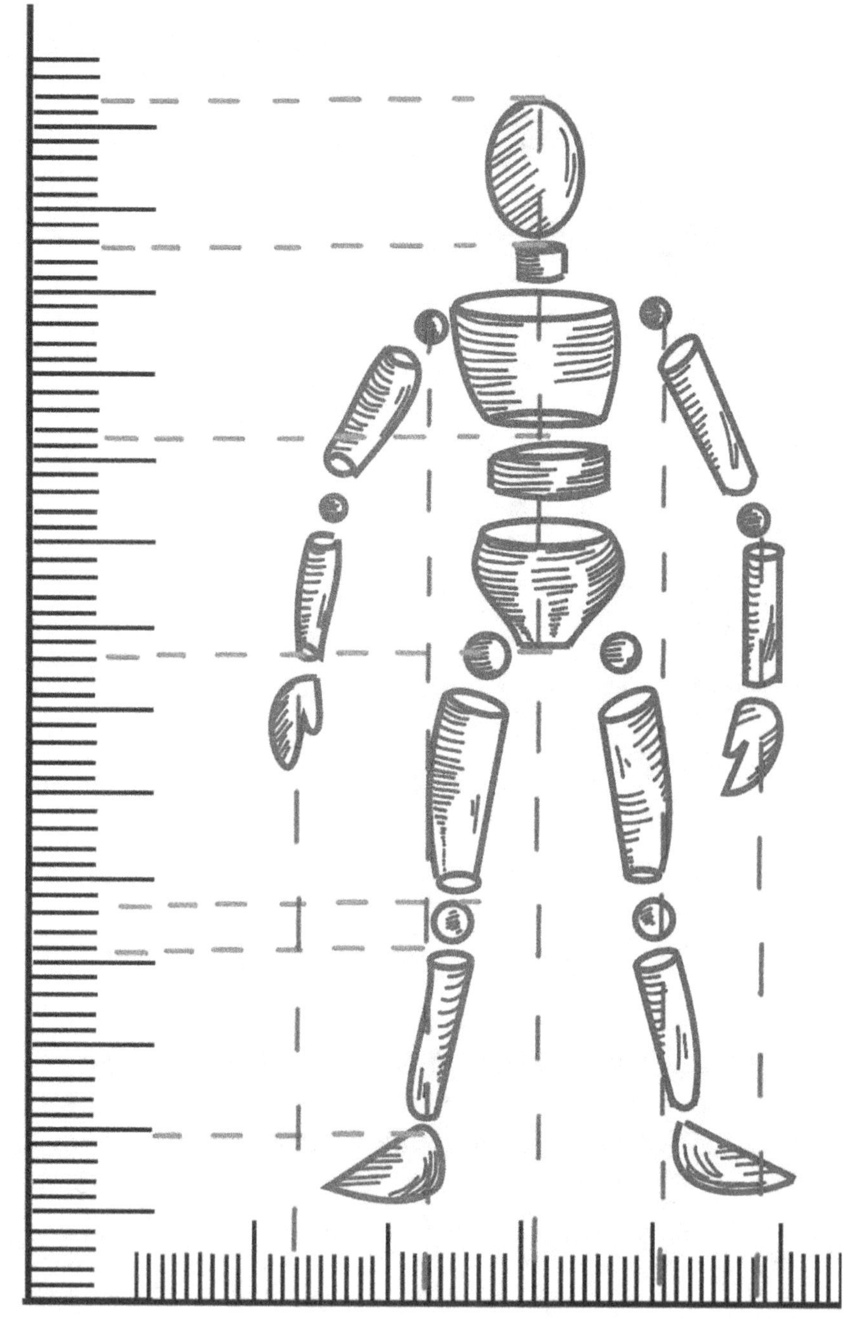

Wooden Mannequin

Male figure

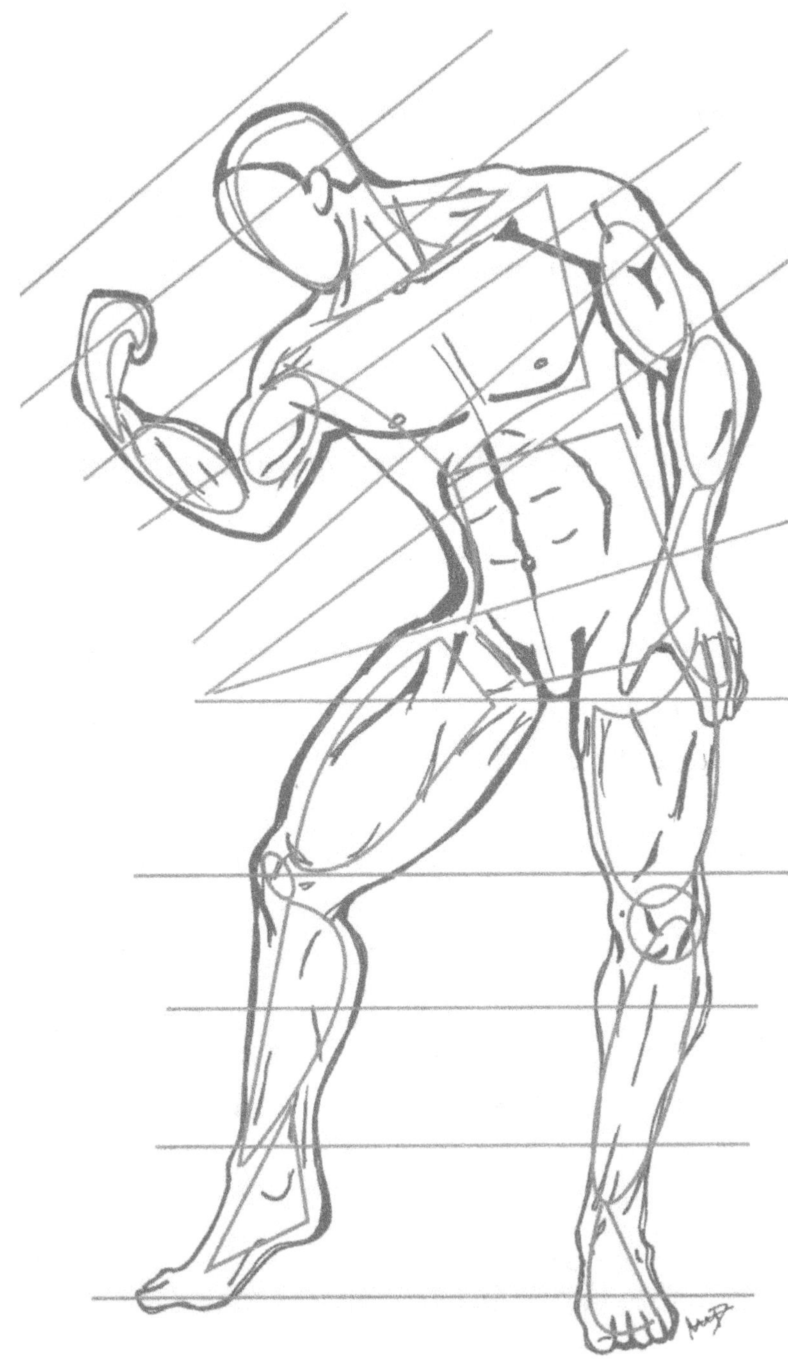

- The Male is broad in the shoulder and narrow at the hips unlike female.

- Male has less fat tissue than female.

- Male have muscular and skeletal prominence.

- Male structure is usually taller in comparison to female.

- Male facial feature are crude and not at all delicate.

- Male have a distinct Adam's apple

- Male have a short neck

- Muscle bulk is prominent in shoulders and chest in male.

- Male chest is usually flat.

- Male waist is lower than the females

- Male jaw is prominent with angular and generous.

- The angle of the legs from the hips to the knee is lesser compared to females.

- Male skeleton is larger and muscular arms and legs.

Male figure in standing

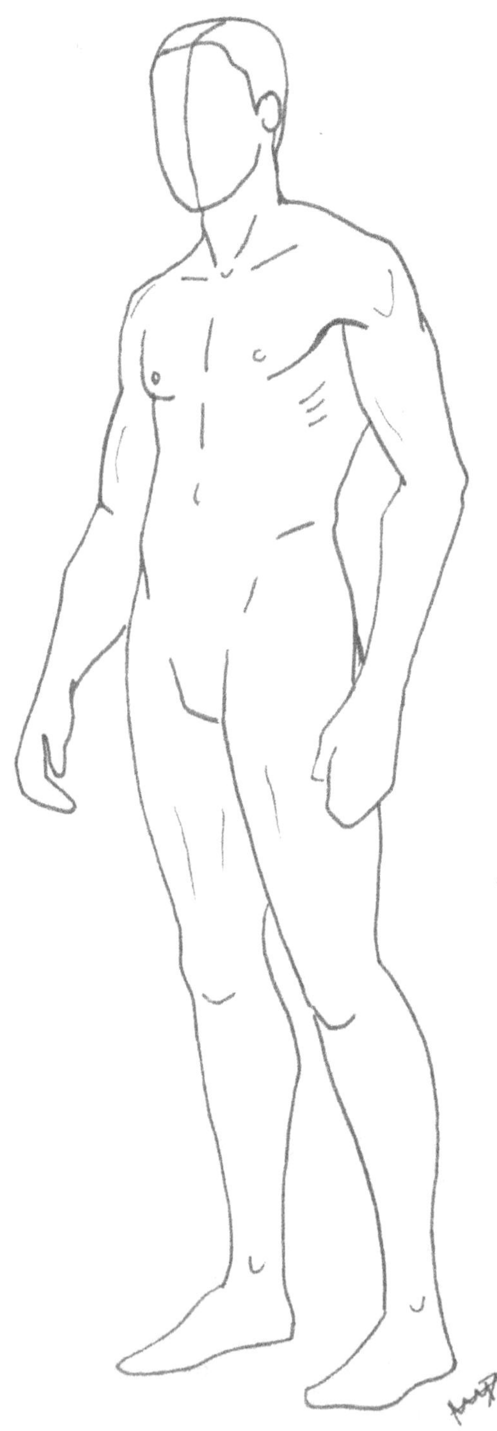

One advantage with the male figure is even with small mistakes won't be evident.

When coming to male figure I would just like to say two words
- *Angular*
- *Muscular*

As mentioned in the early section get your proportions right. One more advantage with male figure is that it doesn't require that artists focus on facial details.

Once you understand the inner structure you are good to go...

The line that marks the spine should be the ***axis of the symmetry,*** so that you can place body parts on the either side of that axis.

When you do drawing of a live model it is important to draw and practice hips in isolation.

Understand the nature and tilt of hip bone, so that you can capture the pose accurately.

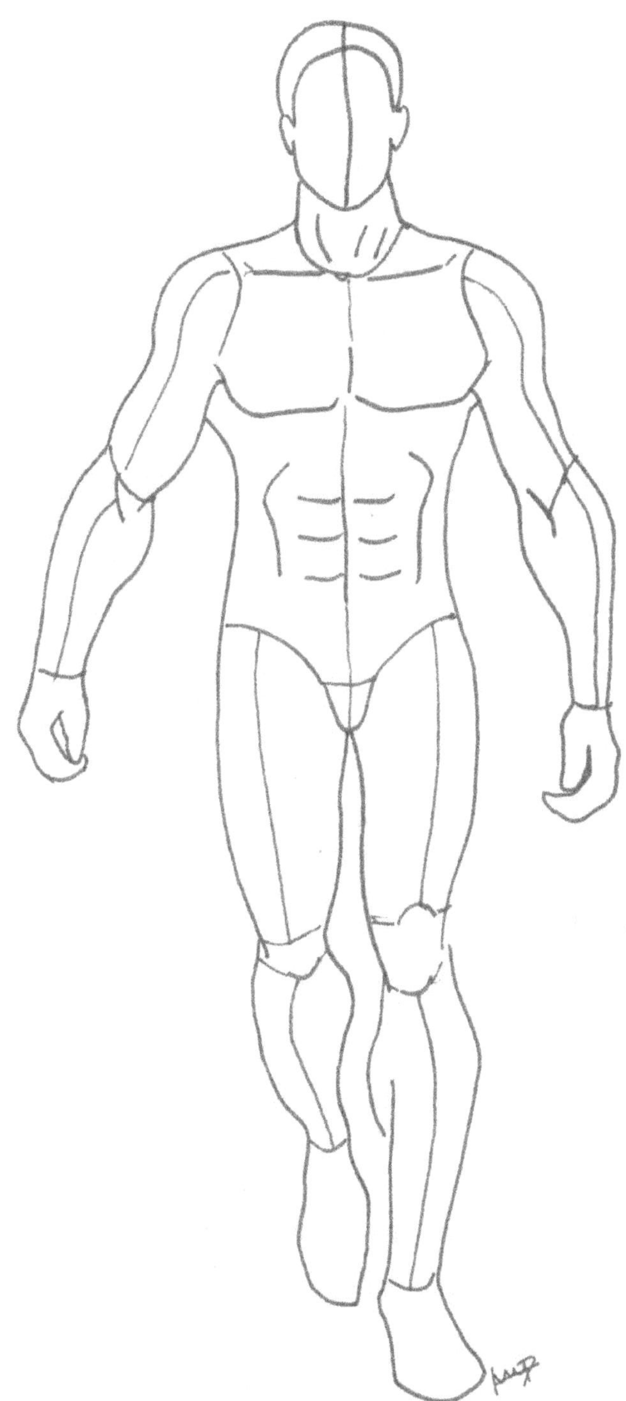

Notice the flow of lines depicted here.

Notice
- *How the central axis of torso (line of action) is arranged*
- *How the surrounding lines of rhythmic movement are arranged.*

Always see figure as a whole and not get carried away by fine details like position of hand or the shape of nose.

Always address the detailing part only when you have drawn a general outline of the model and proportions have come correct with form being satisfactory.

A geometric drawing requires a simple treatment with definitive strokes.

So key take away should be, Always concentrate on the posture, proportions and don't worry too much about deformity.

Try to understand what is hidden underneath every pose.

Try to draw contours as it is one of the most important exercise for practice. (always use fine pencil for contour)

For contour line, it should be un-broken, continuous, overlapping lines and done free handedly.

Keep doing this until you get the complete contour of the figure.

"Art is never finished,
 Only abandoned"
                    - Leonardo Da Vinci

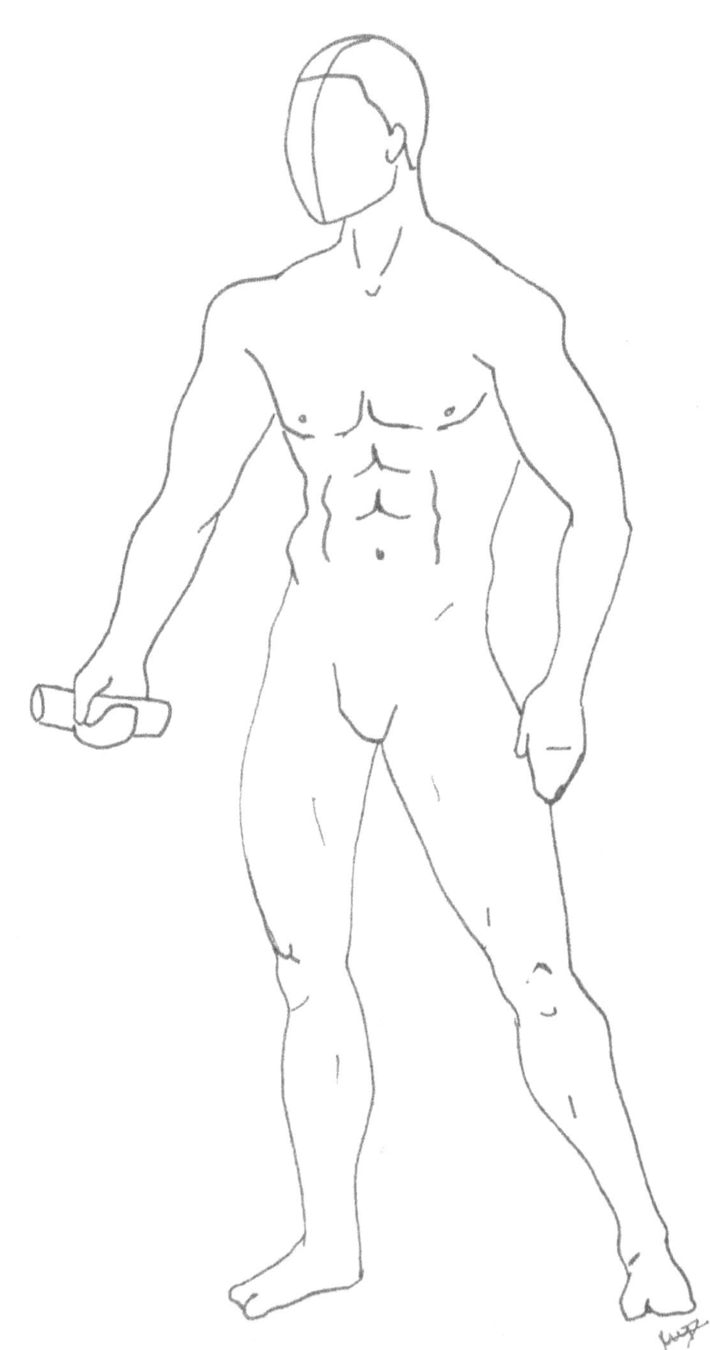

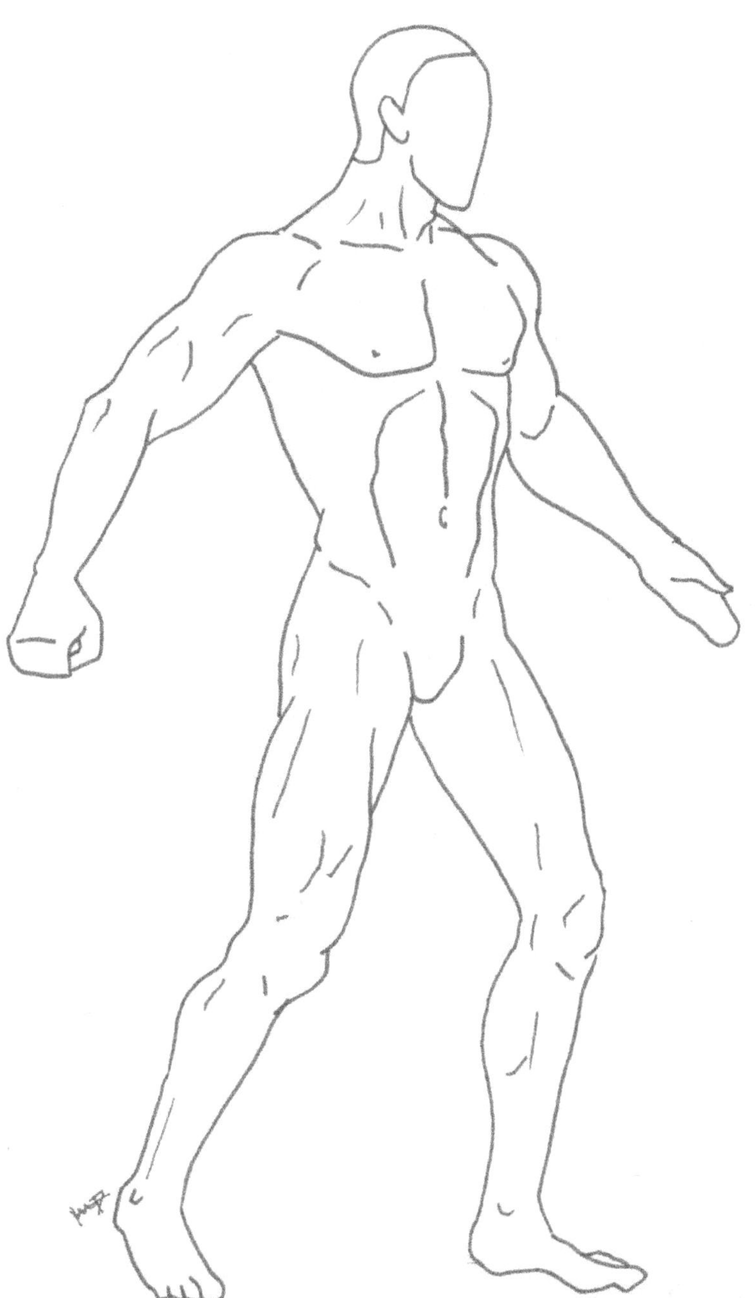

Male figures are usually stiff and less expressive compared to the females.

A drawing is ill proportioned if its head appears big or when arm is short or long, any deviation from normal proportion is considered as abnormal.

Determine any sense of movement presented by the standing figures body.

"I saw the angel in the marble and carved until I set him free"
-Michelangelo

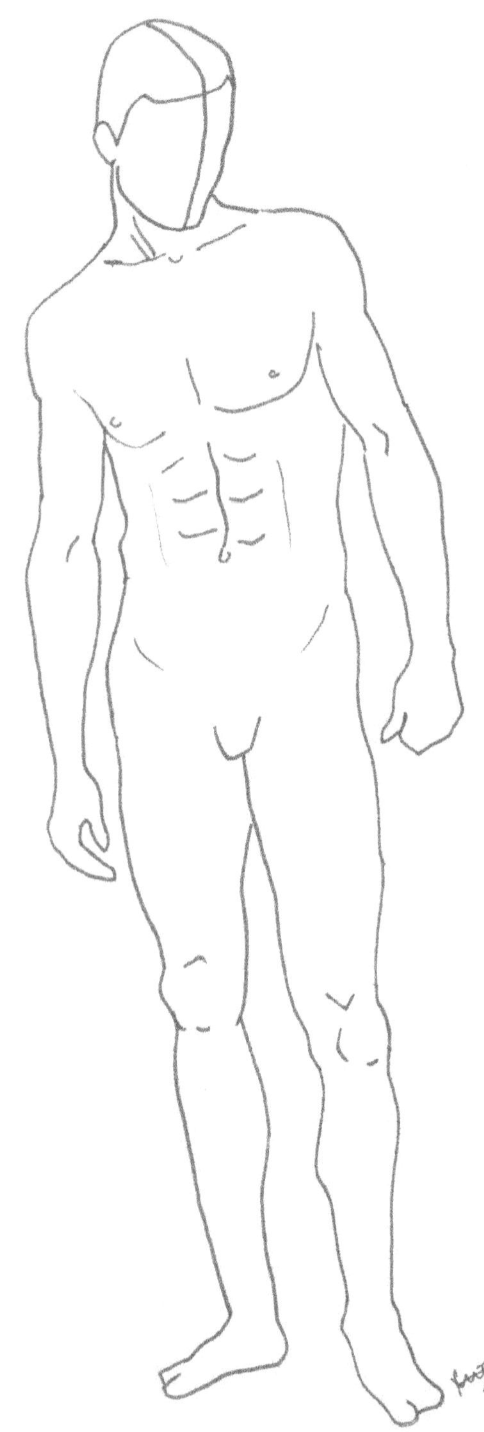

Pelvis is one of the main element in the human figure.

Pelvic area is shaped like a truncated pyramid with a narrow vertex and a big base.

Male pelvis is larger and less wider than that of females pelvis.

Legs are cylinders which gets narrower as we go the bottom.

Arms are also cylindrical forms but the degree of narrowing is not the same when compared to the legs.

Look at the position of the shoulder and its tilt in comparison to the plane of the ground level.

Head tilt and position of arms help in identifying the attitude of the model.

"Good artist copy, Great artist steal" -Pablo Picasso

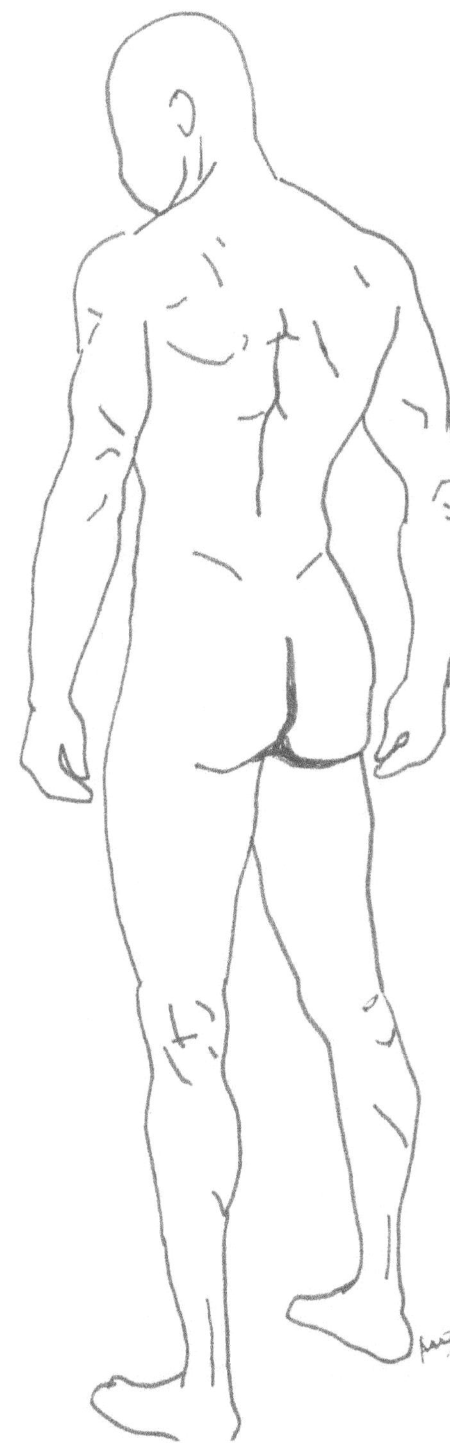

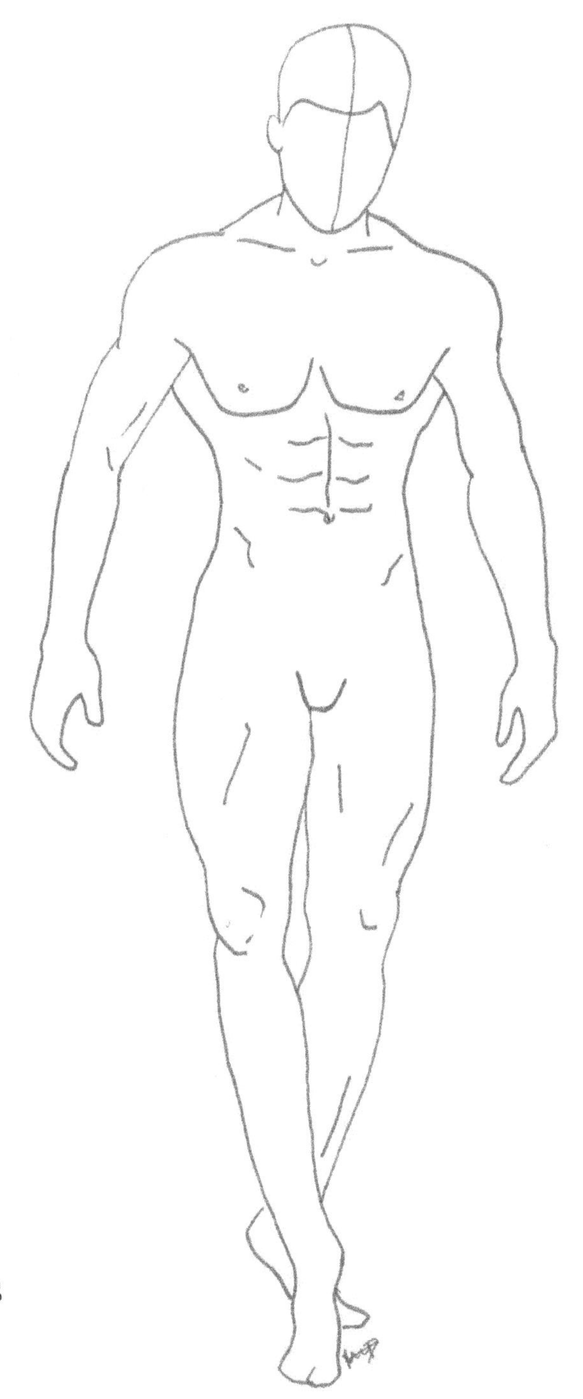

Start from very simple outline of the body so that you can make geometric sketch of the body.

Keeping it as simple as possible and not deviating from the structure of the model is very much necessary step.

Don't get carried away by minute details instead work on the gross details.

Understand the simplicity of the pose of the model here with head slightly down, arms apart and legs crossed.

Here the model is seen standing with both his arms resting on his waist and both legs are apart,

Usually when the model is tired standing for a long time, they choose this pose.

Understanding that the model is tired standing for a long time is very important step because that is the gesture of the model.

Everyone can see that the model is in the standing position, but not all can capture this gesture unless you are an artist.

"To paint the most terrific thing that there is but to do it well is very difficult"
- Frida Kahlo

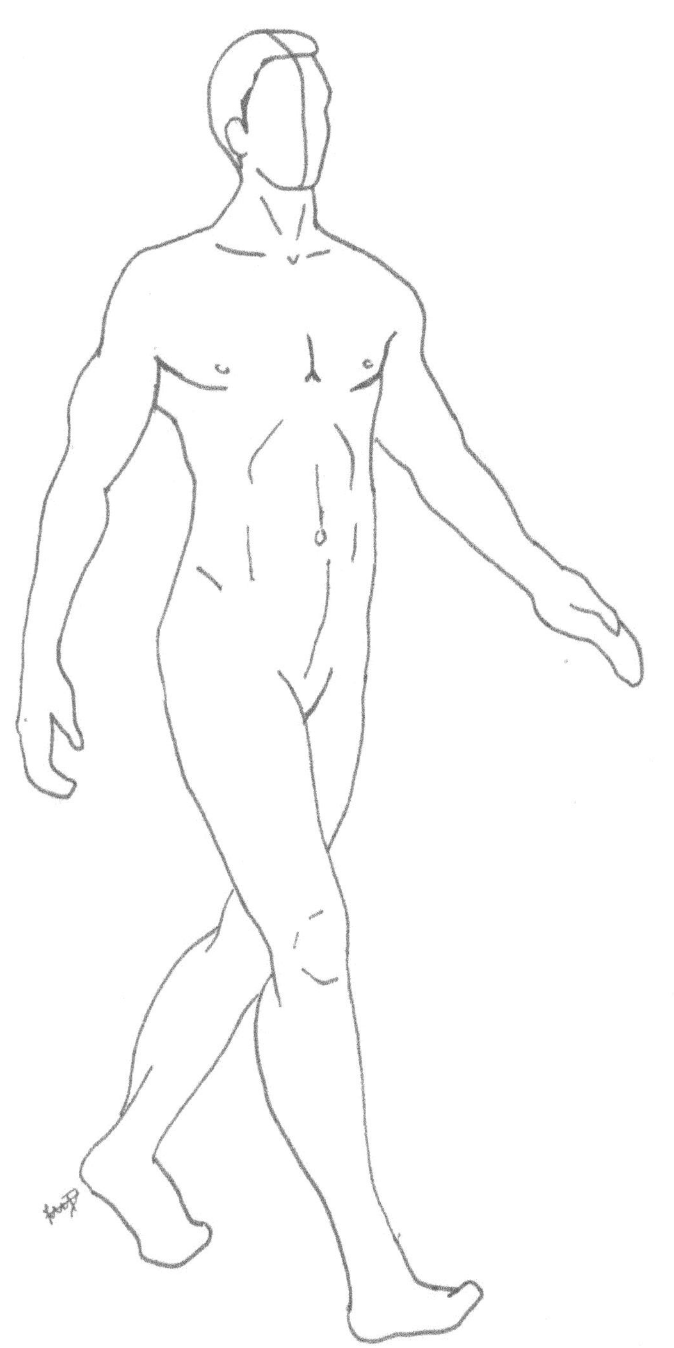

Feel the momentum of gestural movement of a walking male model.

This illustration should help you give a clear idea of how gesture is expressed in a figure drawing.

Proportion should not be varied and should be kept unaltered as much as possible.

"A painting is not a picture of experience, but is the experience"

-Mark Rothko

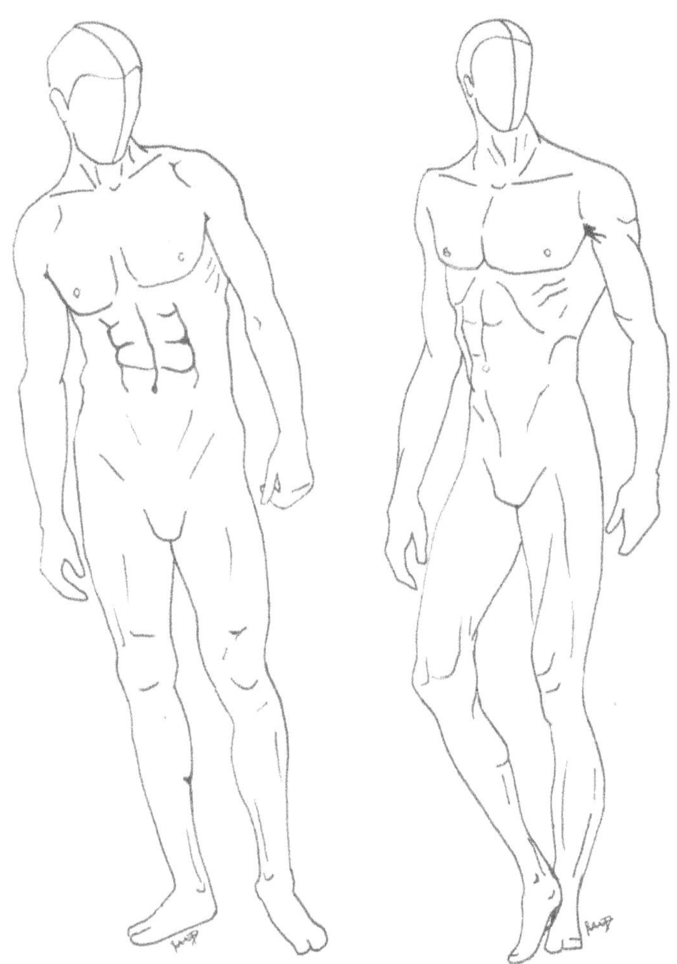

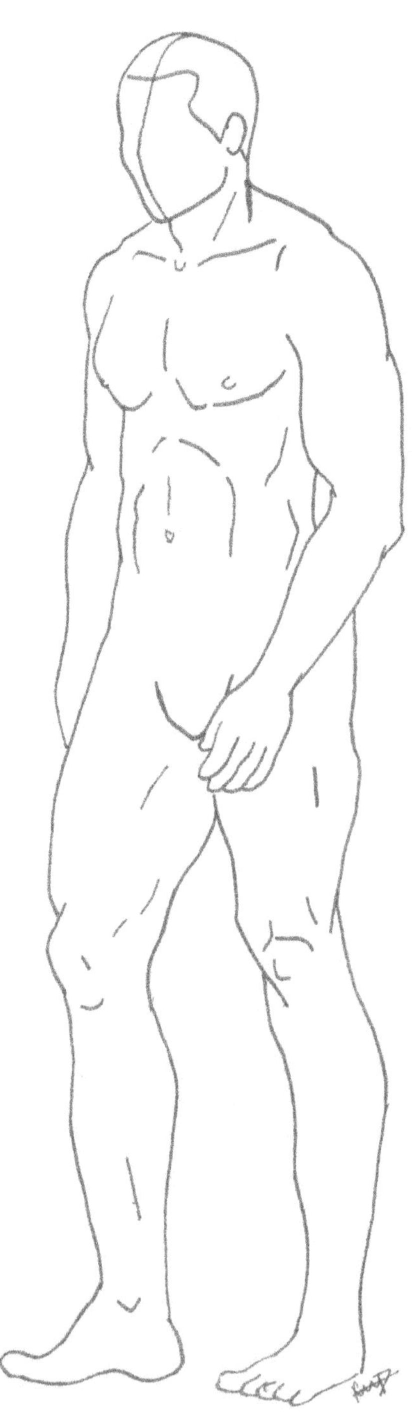

The same model in different angles may look like two different person, but it's completely fine because that's how it works. In early stages of drawing, this is the common problem bothering people. Just ensure you get proportions right, the rest doesn't matter much.

" To be an artist is to believe in life"   -Henry Moore

Mastery of line and its control is very crucial step because

- *It creates a sense of direction*

- *It creates vital essence of figure*

- *It defines contours of volume*

Don't miss out on important land-marks while you are working on figure study.

Landmark can be divided as
- Skeletal landmark
- Muscular landmark
- Surface landmark

"A beautiful body perishes,
 But a work of art does not"
                    - Leonardo Da Vinci

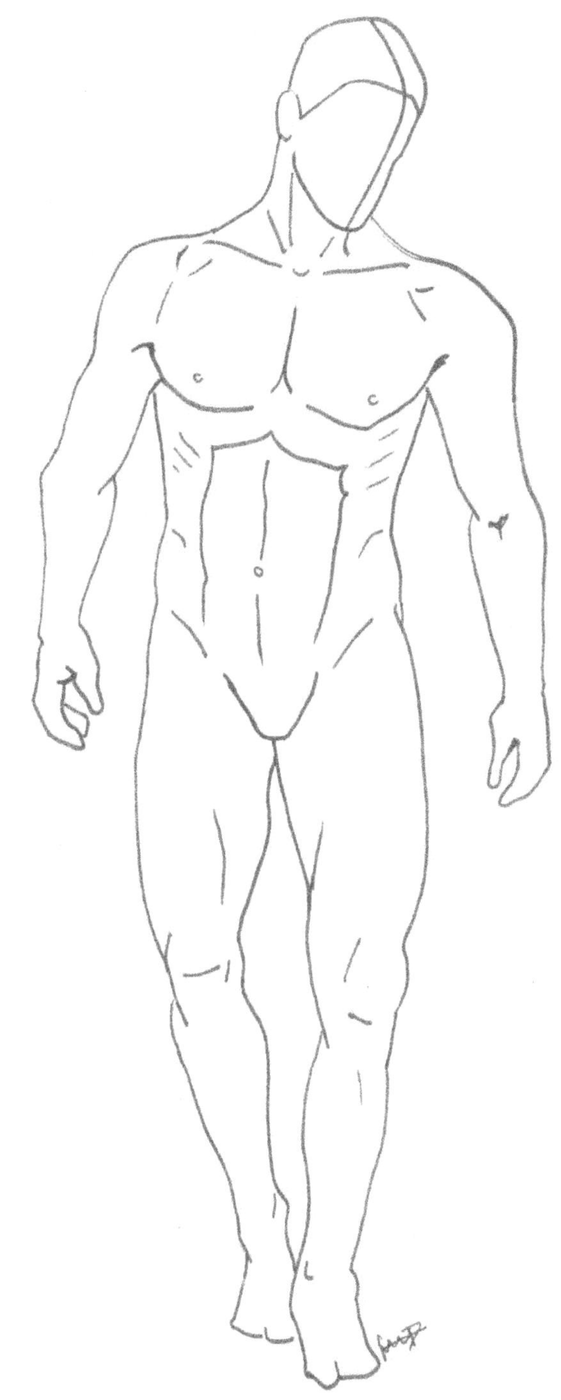

This is a lean figure compared to muscular forms described in previous pages.

I have drastically reduced the muscle mass and added details like narrow. Experiment with different body shapes such as obese, fit for, lean forms.

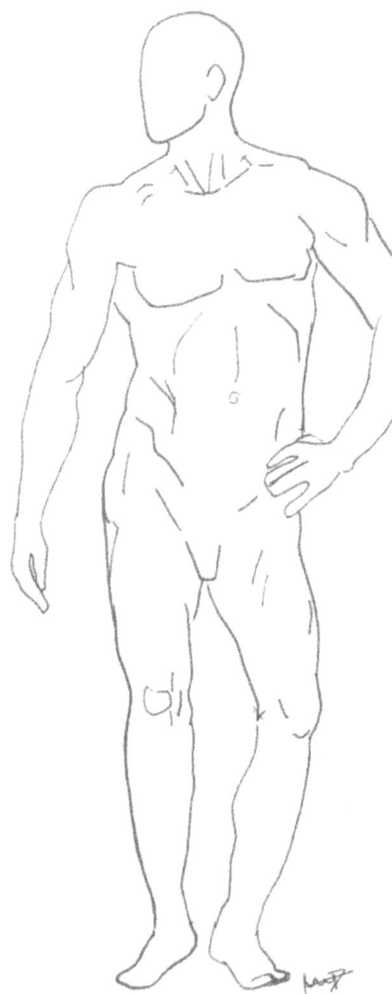

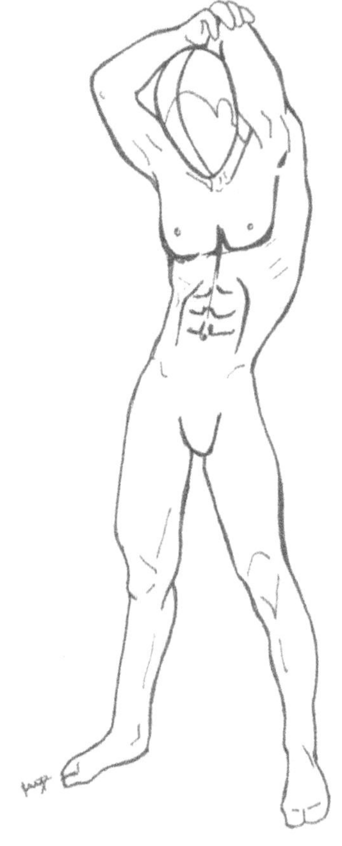

When ever you are trying to show the three dimensional aspect of the figure pretend you are an ant crawling over the surface of the model. Now you can visualize the form better.

Important landmarks
- Sternum
- Naval
- Armpit
- Knee
- Chin
- Ankle
- Elbows

"Every artist was first an amateur
-Ralph Waldo Emerson

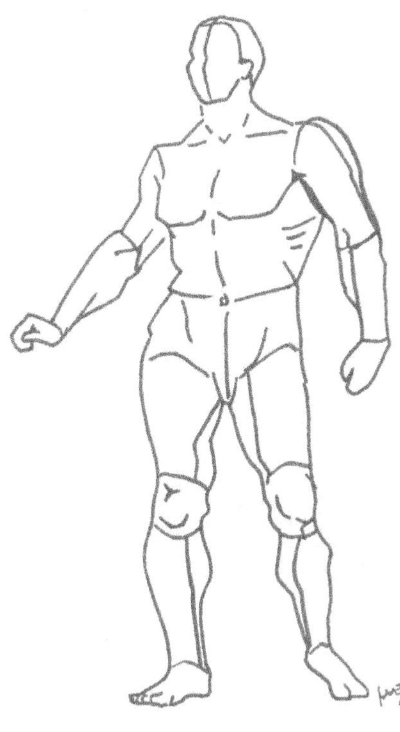

Here I've just defined the shape of the model in form of sharp edges.

Male body is angular and not at all delicate like female.

Just focus on getting structure something like this and work on it later.

You need not always make a sketch look complicated, sometimes its just better to keep it as simple as possible.

Sometimes all eyes needs to visualize is the essence of the drawing rather than the minute detailing.

I don't mean to tell you people to abandon the sketches in the early stages, but for a beginner artist you need not focus on minute detailing. The more the number of sketches you do, the better.

"The great artist is the simplifier"
                                    -Vincent Van Gogh

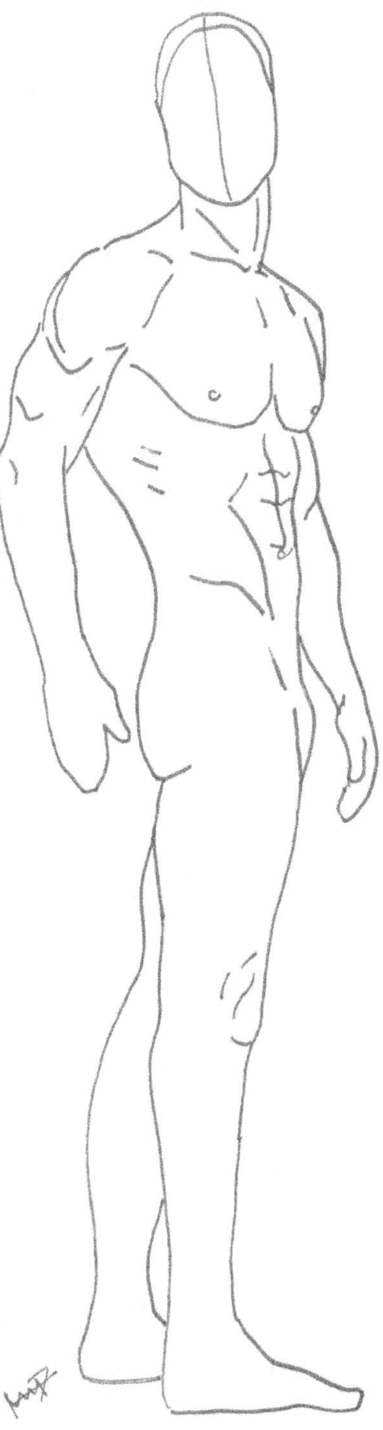

Male Figure in sitting

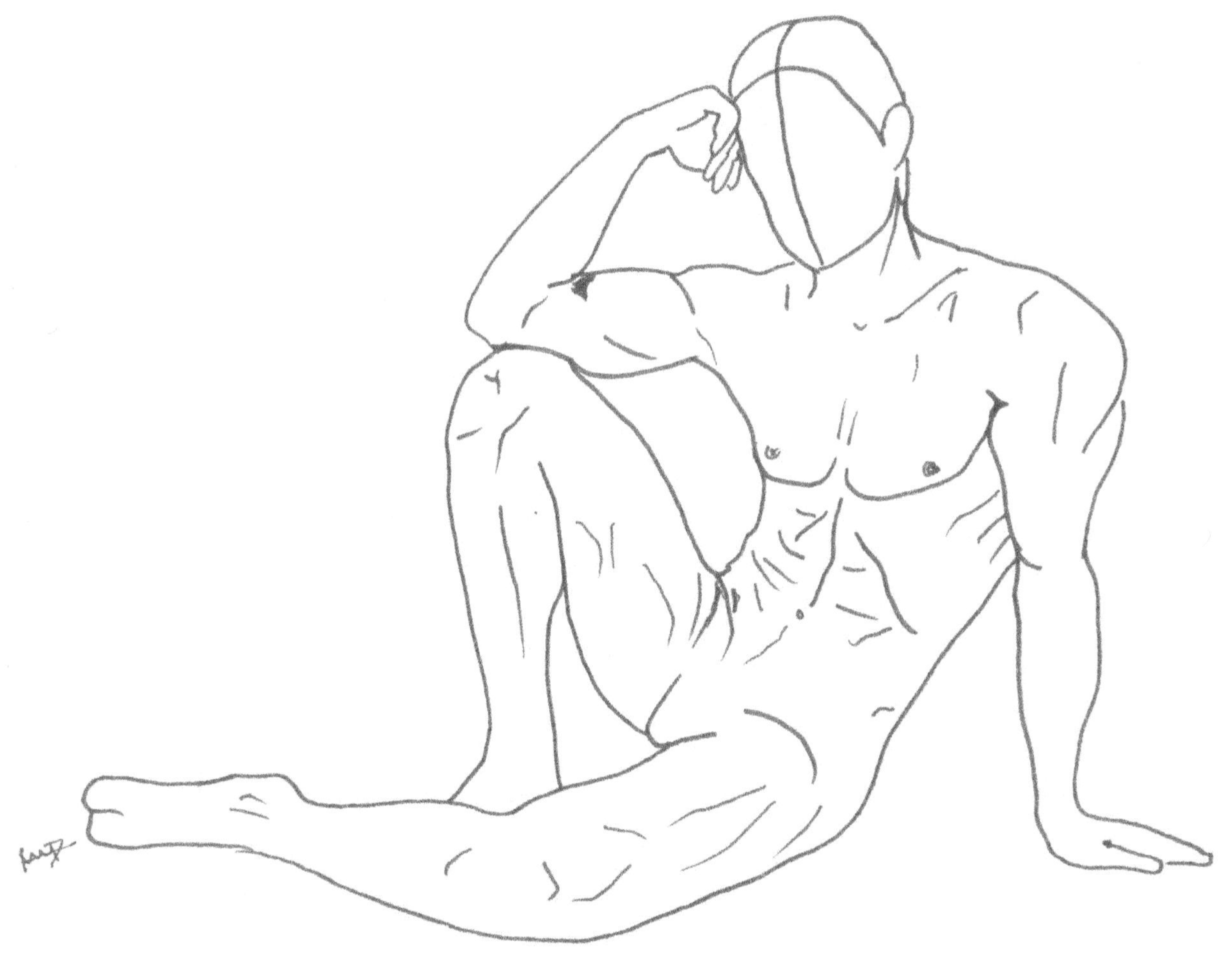

When drawing a seated figure, the weight of the body should be properly distributed among the legs and supporting arms as shown here. Though the muscles may not appear evidently because the body will be relaxed in seated position, capture any details of the muscle which you can.

When constructing a pose, always exaggerate the line of force and later take it to more realistic position.

Any kind of methods require great deal of practice and not getting the desired results always ends up in disappointment. Don't get discouraged.

Regardless you acquire the experience in the practice.

"It's good as an artist to always remember to see things in a new, weird way"
-Tim Burton

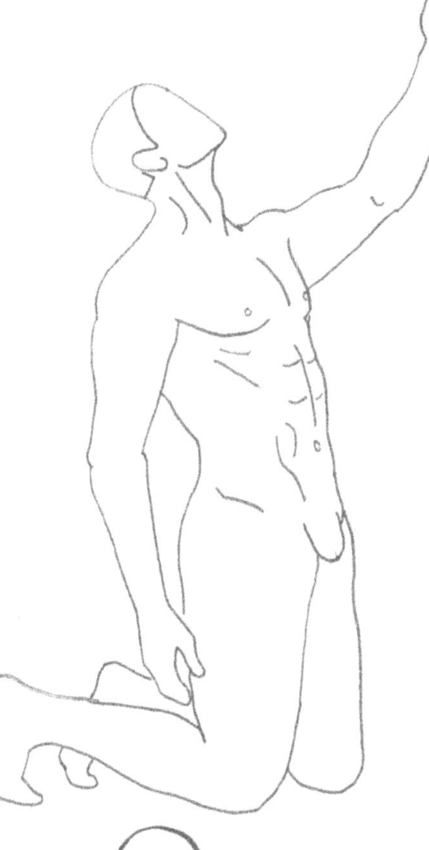

Sometimes the unfinished hands make sense in case of nude drawing.

One doesn't look into the details of finger compared to the other parts of the body.

Notice the muscular arms of this model which is some what relaxed yet its bulky form appears significant.

It may sound silly, but it is necessary to *learn the names of at least prominent muscles, its shape and mass*.

Muscles get tensed when engaged in action.

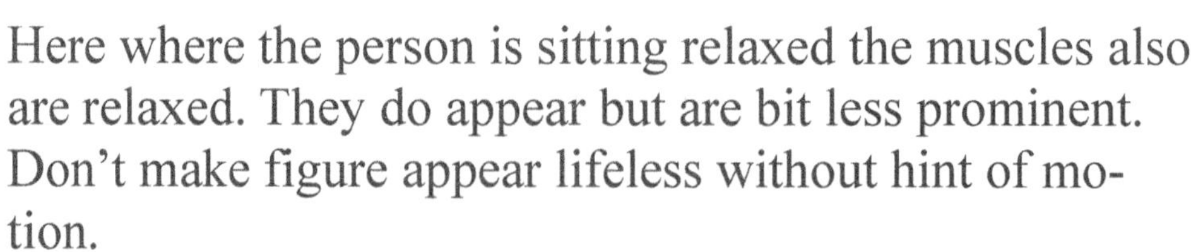

Here where the person is sitting relaxed the muscles also are relaxed. They do appear but are bit less prominent. Don't make figure appear lifeless without hint of motion.

"Learn the rules like a pro, so you can break them like an artist" -Pablo Picasso

Male Figure in flexed posture

Muscle is what which gives body its contours

Shape of human body depends upon its structure, so artist knowledge about anatomy will come in handy.

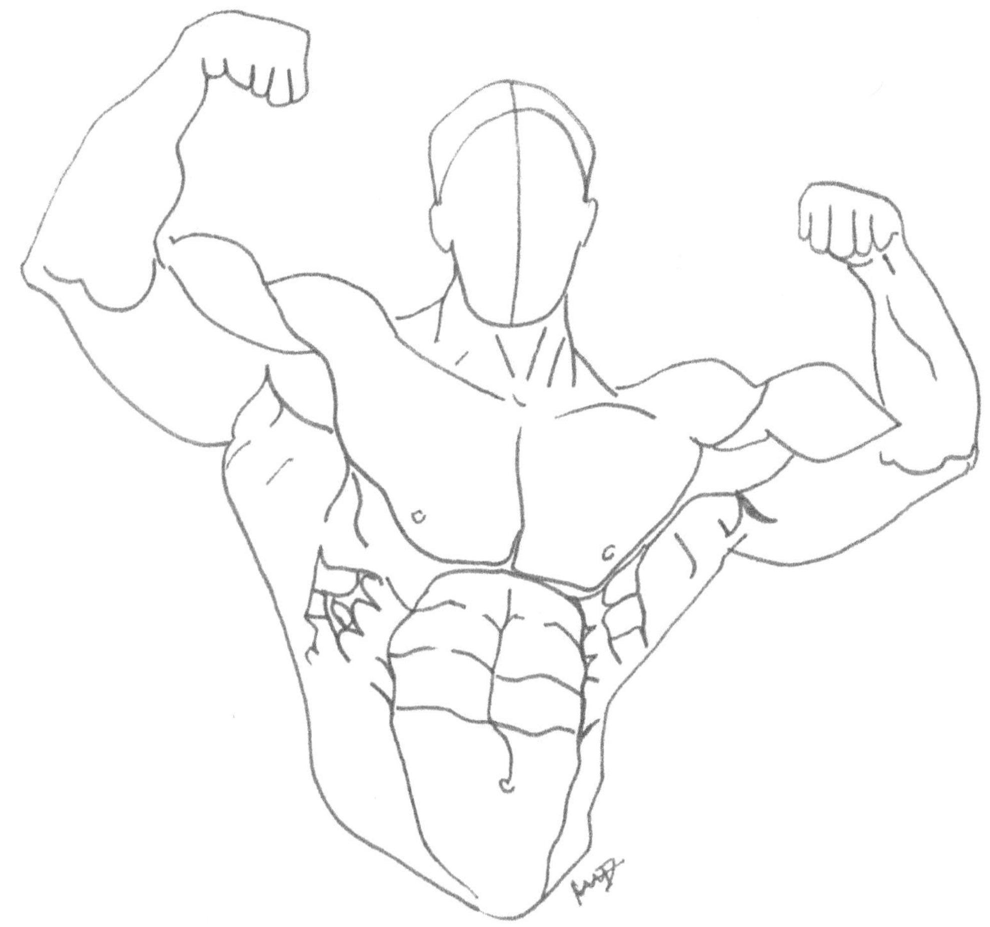

Shape of the body is defined by bone structure & the layers of muscles covering it

Notice the distribution of volume, thorax shape, the form, the muscle bulk and symmetry. The musculature with muscle mass is main feature represented here.

"The principles of true art is not to portray, but to evoke"
-Jerzy Kosinski

The adjacent figure here appear to be narrated by a strange equilibrium predominated by the action, in an motion propelled by a force that unites all the elements of figure and adds meaning to it when we understand rhythm of the figure.

A figure drawing should always look like lines in a poetry intertwined and connected to each other and finally ending up beautifully creating appeal in the viewers.

" Have no fear of perfection,
 You'll never reach it"
                    -Salvador Dali

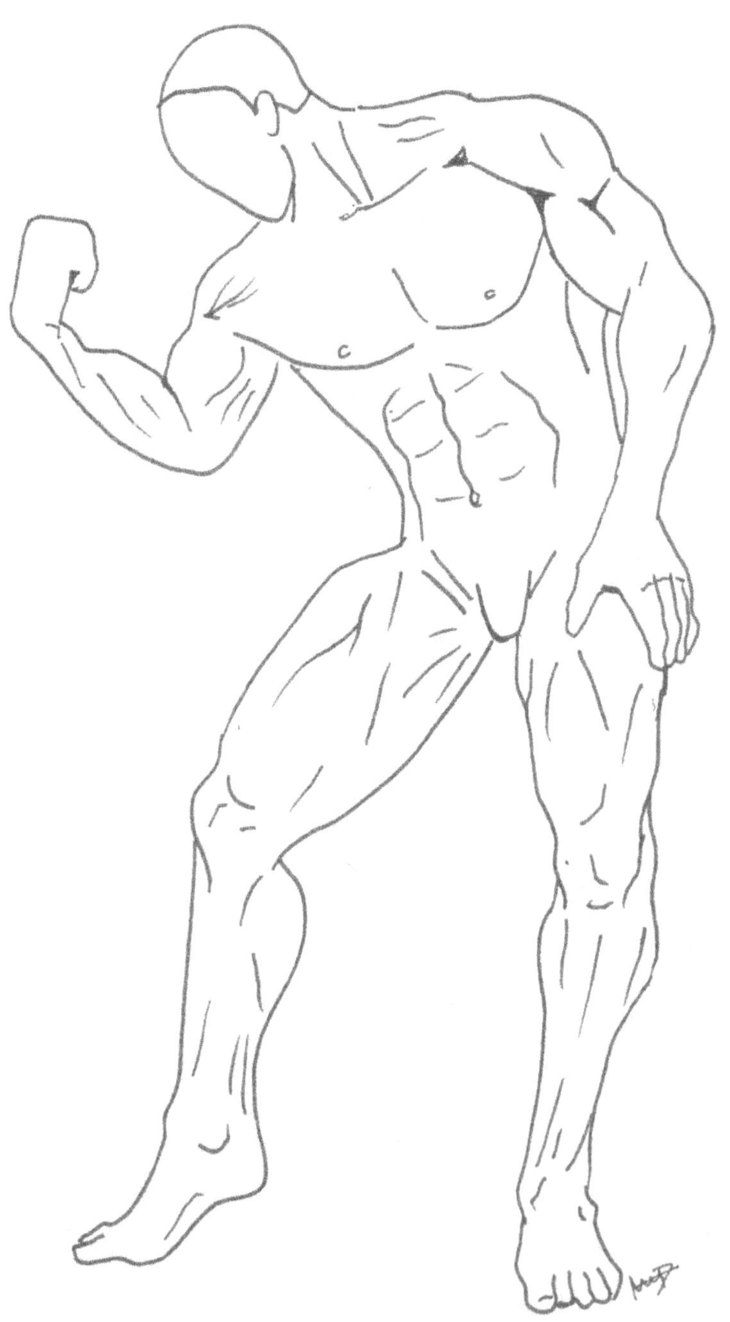

When you build a pose, it is always preferred that you exaggerate the line of force .

Here the figure is rigid with conventional pose but equally trying to radiate its presence and energy shown by those detailed musculature.

Notice how additional lines indicates volume of the muscles, its stretch and bulk of masses

"A good artist has less time than the ideas"
        -Martin Kippenberger

- Muscles are driving force of the body.

- Muscles put the figure in action.

- Never get carried away by the vision of movement and forget all the basic consideration.

- Use eraser for connecting errors and to lighten.

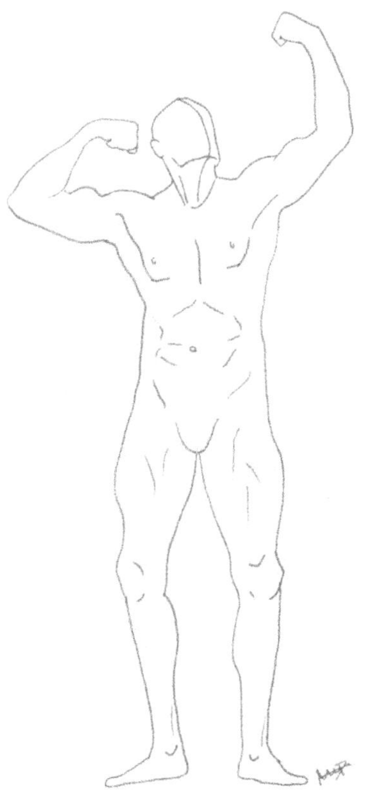

Always understand body posture first.

Here the model is flexing his arms and is standing with a twisted torso.

Though I have stressed only about the proportion and form of the model in this entire book, only by using basic general outline one cannot add volume and mass by using mere lines.

Male Figure in action

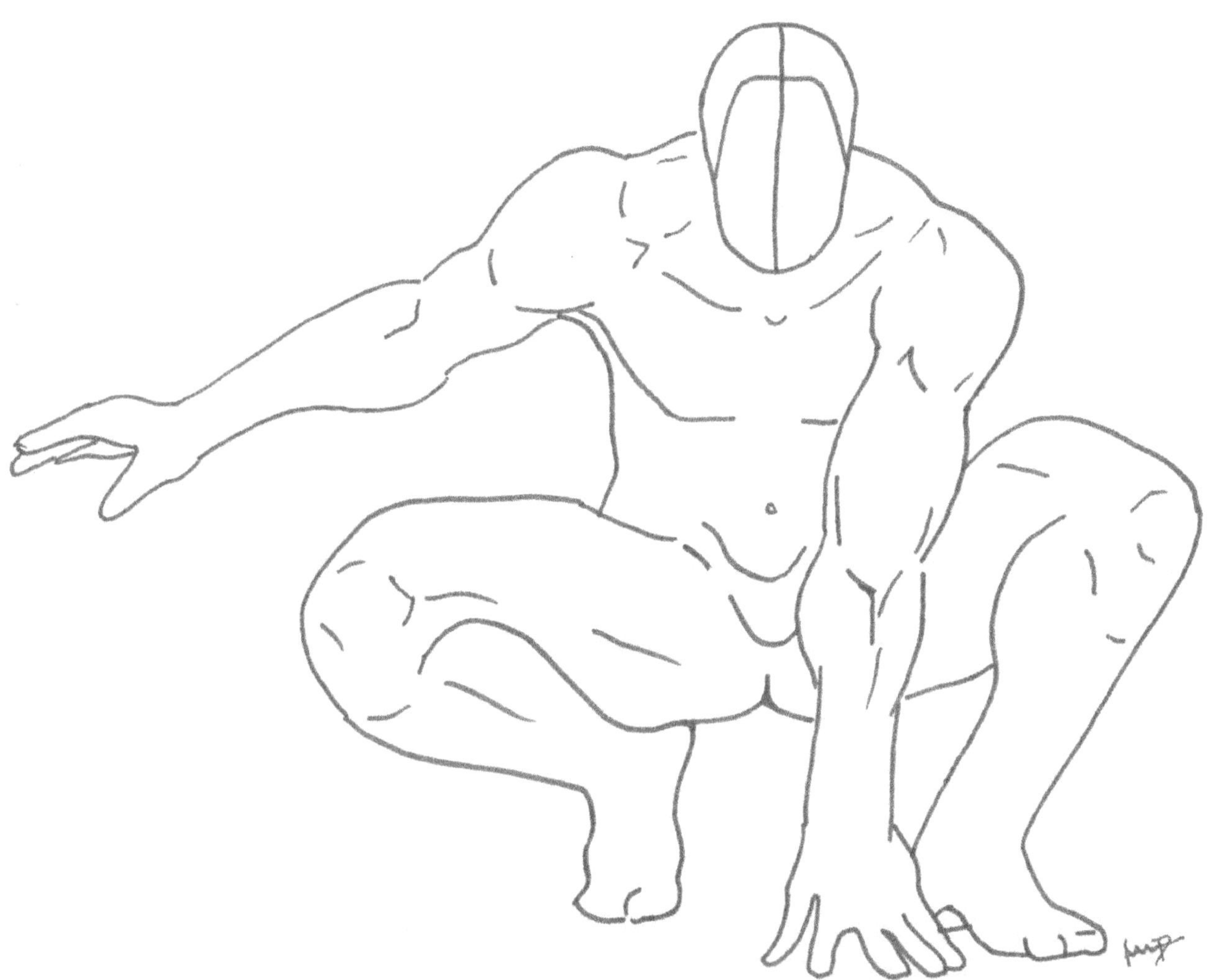

Learn to draw the gesture of the figure by keen observation because when figure is in action you won't get much time to observe model fixed in one pose.

Always try to capture the intention of the figure.

Males legs have prominent musculature and less delicacy.

Males calves are prominent and less narrowing at the ankle.

Geometrical configuration of the foot is pretty much similar to that of the hands but the digits of foot are several smallish ovals for toes.

While drawing the figure in action *the lines of strength* should be very expressive as I've shown in this sketch.

"A picture is a poem without words"

   -Horace

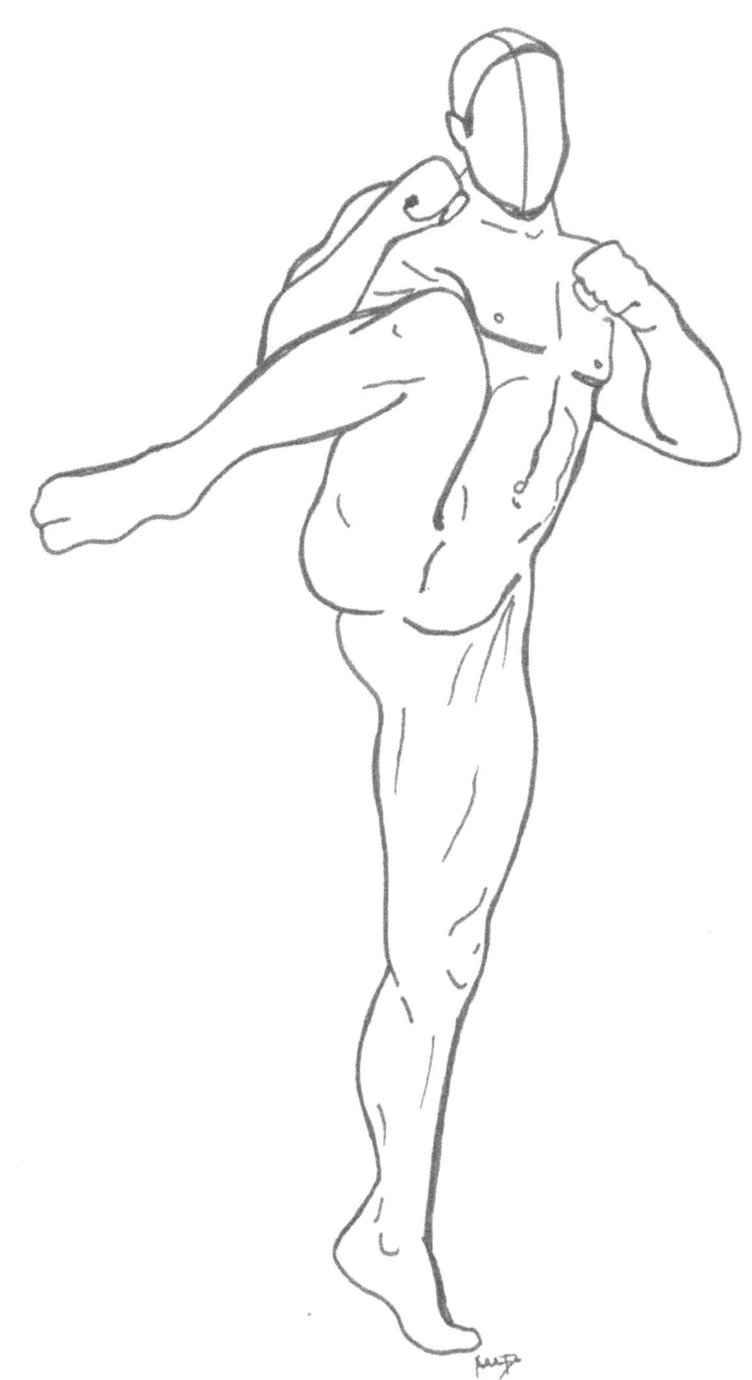

The muscles in the lower limb presents as a complex form, but upon doing detailed analysis, you can identify each one of them

Lower limbs = thighs + knees + calves

There are no limits to the possibilities for creating good, attractive, unusual and different striking poses.

Each model has their own way of walking, posing, sitting.

"Creating art is painful. It takes time, practice and courage to stand alone"

-Maria Semple

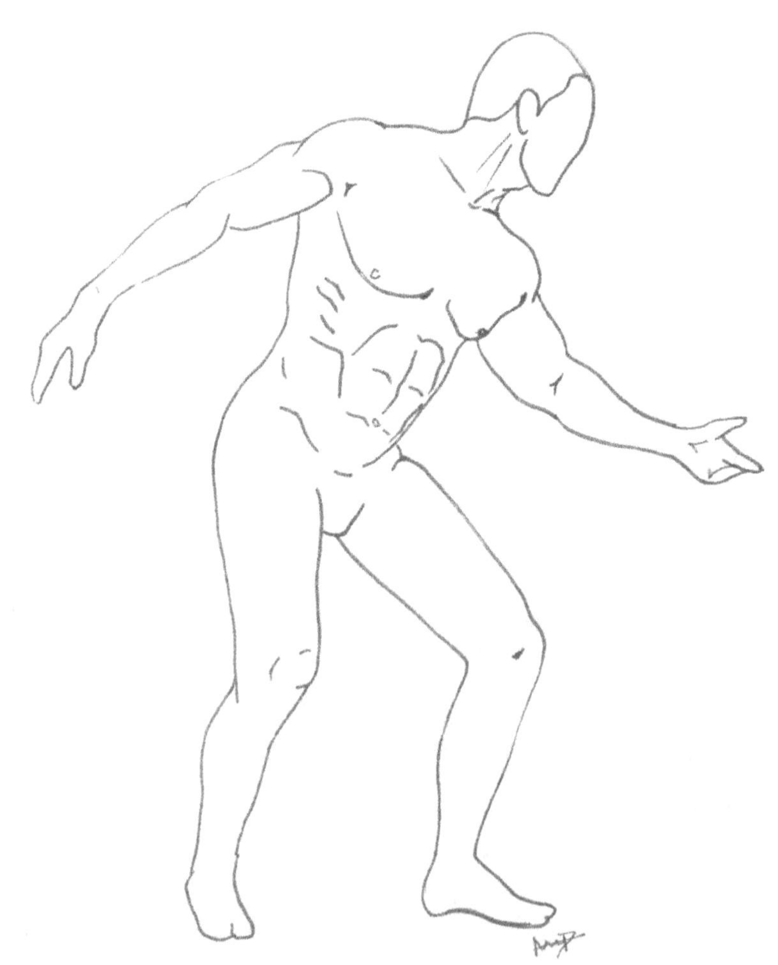

Knee joint is never located in the midway of the leg instead a bit further down.

Therefore when you draw thigh make sure its lengthier than the calves.

When drawing figure bin action just put aside pro-portion for the sake of spontaneity, freshness and the rhythm, even if it deforms some part of model.

A quick and interesting drawing is always appreci-ated the most, every movement of model expresses something

" Creativity is greatest rebellion in existence" - Osho

A running is always amazing thing to draw

Firstly the figure in running is where almost all the muscles are put into use.

The toned rigid appearance is mainly due to the tonic contraction of the muscle

The body in motion attains and changes its posture with every fraction of second.

Notice the main motion occurs at the hip and the legs is usually prominent.

" The world always seems brighter when you've just made something that wasn't there before"
                    -Neil Gaiman

Despite the pose what model assumes when in action, make sure that it is organized within rational and comprehensible order, in such a way that it comforts and appeals eyes

When in action, the figure tends to alters its proportion drastically but its all about fore-shortening. In such cases don't worry too much about measurements and geometry of the figure.

Male figure especially when in action has most expressive appearance and has its own mechanical way to describe itself.

When drawing the torso its line tilts in opposite direction.

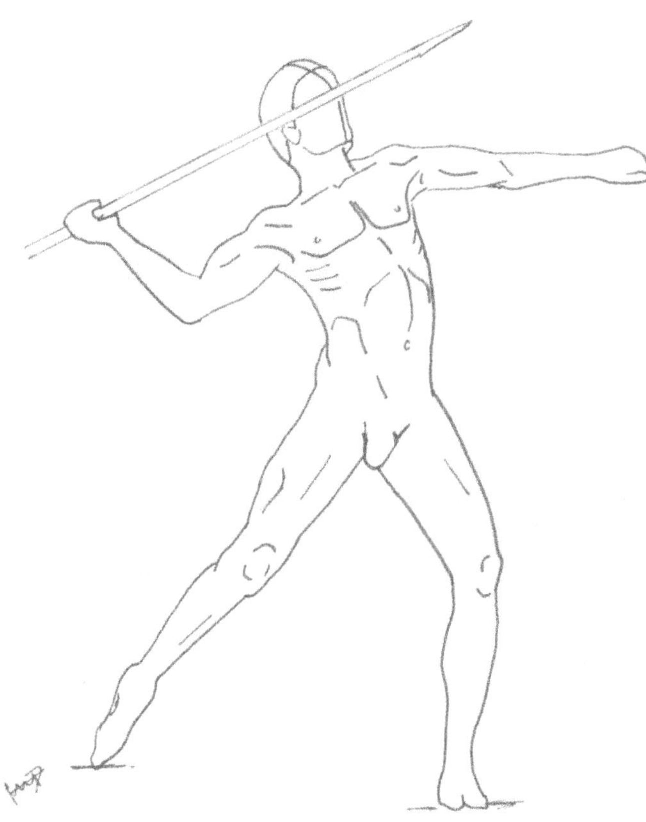

This is a forced pose represented here with accentuated slope of lines of shoulder.

Notice outstretching of arm, dragging of legs and tilt of the pelvis.

When model has assumed a complicated posture, the standard law of proportion becomes difficult to apply.

So one must draw figures corresponding to inner structures carefully, adjust proportions and measurements accordingly.

Stability of the figure and its pose is very important when you are drawing a figure and following factors determines it-

- Center of gravity
- Balance
- Weight distribution
- Symmetry of the figure
- Composition

Look carefully how the balance is formed here by the model by standing on the tips of the toe

Always inscribe on the simple geometric shape the pose what model is assuming.

Plot out visual layout in such a way that you feel satisfied and content after looking at it. Make sure viewers look into what you are trying to make them look at by organizing the elements properly.

Analyze weight distribution here where all the weight is transferred to the left leg and entire body gets into that posture to balance itself.

"If you could say it in words, there would be no reason to paint"

-Edward Hopper

Female Figure

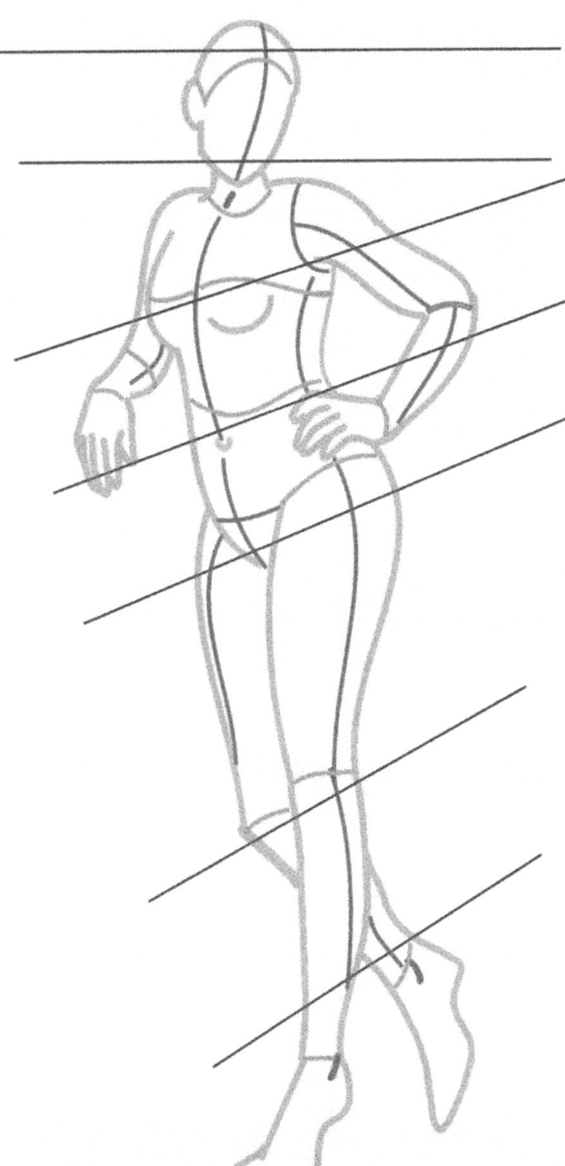

Female figure in standing

Firstly our focus is to get the outline right

This book focuses on getting the outline properly rather than adding lights and tones

With change in the position the body form changes simultaneously

In standing figure unlike other poses , you can use standard eight measurements easily

Three ways a figure can stand
1. All weight on one leg and other leg balances the body
2. All weight on one leg and other leg is raised
3. All weight distributed on both legs equally

Varying position gives different shape to hips and shoulder depending on the stance

There is no absolute formula to get proportions precisely right.

Human error are bound to happen and I would consider it to be normal.

We can't expect the unit of measurement such as head units to be precisely accurate and perfect.

Observation is the key factor for a better outcome.

Practice over time lets you realize that our great ancestors didn't stress much about ratios and proportions.

TRIAL AND ERROR is the best approach to learn and develop any skills according to me.

Look at the shape body moulds itself into as in this standing posture.

Understand the structure to form a perspective .

Line has 3 definite character
1.Length
2.Direction
3.Curvature

These 3 character varies from one to other form.

Let's focus mainly on how to get the outline right.

As a beginner, your at most worry is supposed to be how to get the basic figure right

There are two kinds of drawing
Solid drawing
Linear drawing

Solid drawing is three dimensional having mass and is bulky.

As shown in figure here , this is the basic structure of female in her standing posture with arms relaxed by the sides of the body

Here we first need to apply the proportion rule as discussed previously.

 Note the positioning of the arm and tilt of the head

Legs are still crossed and the body seems elongated towards left side.

 Study the landmarks like elbow, neck carefully, this will keep your figure more lively.

Carefully note that *central line passing through the body* is not a straight line here. It looks curved, more like English alphabet "S"

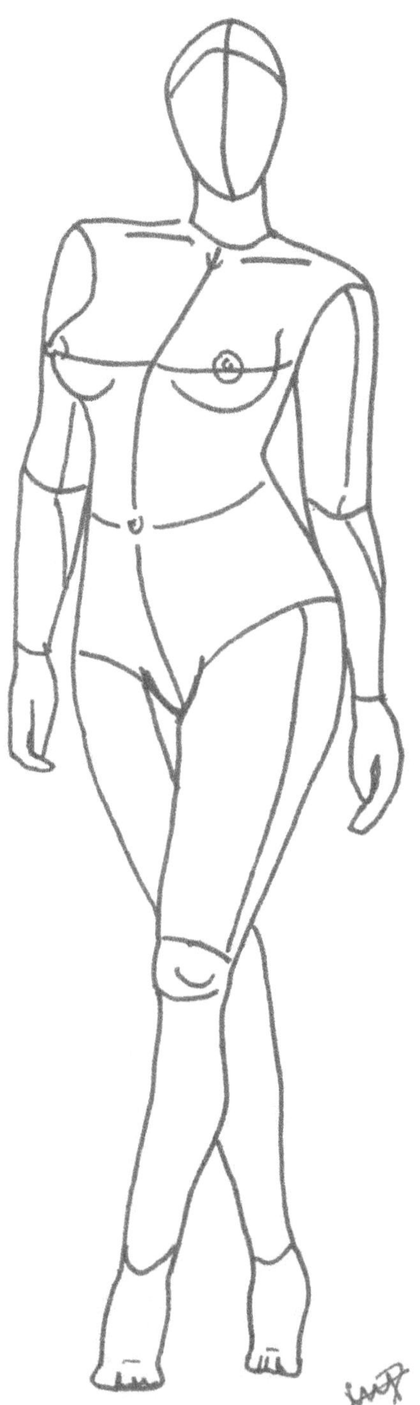

Even without the study of the anatomy, your awareness of body's bony landmark and shapes of the muscles will help you to a certain extent.

If you are studying anatomy, start by familiarizing yourself with basic shapes of bones and muscles.

Keep a small journal of A5 size with you and do sketches during waiting time in the queue or when you are in line for something or waiting for someone or any similar situation. Try 1-2 sketches per week even if complete the sketch, it's ok.

Even incomplete sketches have great appeal.

Females naturally have more fat tissue than male covering the skeletal and muscular forms. Hence get a soft, rounded look.

NOTICE

- How narrow the shoulder and arms appears
- How wide the hips seems
- How slender the neck is
- How smooth and heavy the buttocks are
- How fine and delicate the facial features are

Breast varies in shape and size. Sideways the breast appears like hemisphere.

Females have that peculiar less angular appearance compared to the male. Also *females have less body hairs.*

When arms are relaxed at the side of the
torso as seen in the sketch on the adjacent
page, Elbows tend to align with the waist,
the wrist tend to align with the center line
of the figure parallel.

Bones of the female are shorter and have
less rough surface than that of the male.

Pelvis in females is broader giving hips a
wider appearance.

Sacrum in female is wide and angles outwards

Female abdomen is more rounded and
thighs are thicker from back to front than
males.

In females there is more fat on the buttocks
giving a greater diameter.

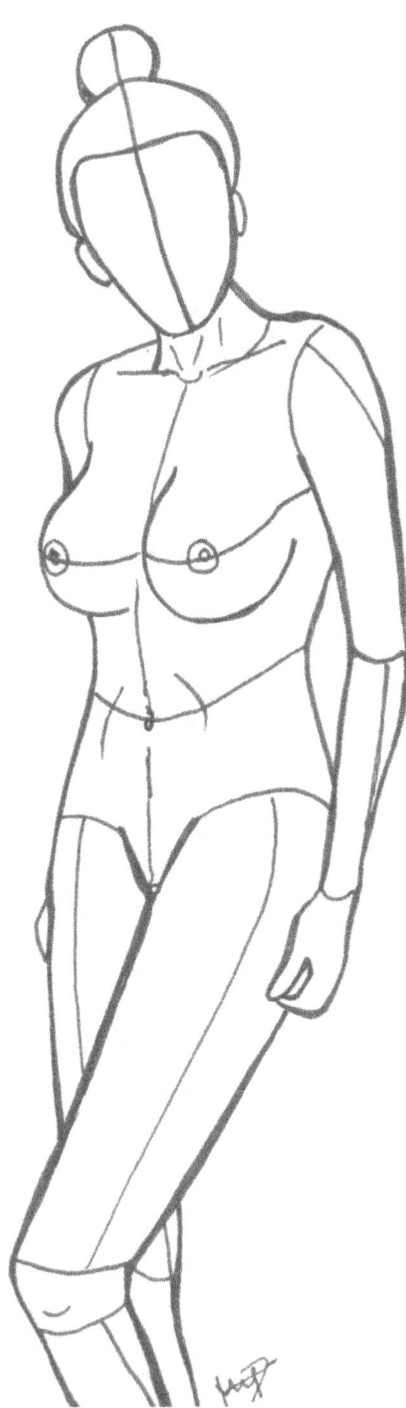

Always work on appreciating THREE DIMEN-SIONAL aspect while drawing the model.

Always consider which view you want to draw
- Frontal view
- Side view
- Backside view
- Oblique view

The line from the nipple to armpit forms the angle separating the chest from body.

Examine this drawing carefully, see overall direction of the curving lines.

Drawing doesn't require too much level of precision. All it needs is
- Observe
- Draw
- Evaluate
- Fix what needs fixing

Even in standing there are uncountable number and varieties of actions which a human figure can do. So easy approach would be to break a form into components. Then add up components and form a figure.

54

Understand the gesture, feel what the model is feeling, the work of her muscles in maintaining the pose, the head tilt, the tilt at the hip.

Understand the whole body, try to see how each body part complement one another.

Life will express itself in each and every part of her body.

And apart from it, the model isn't just standing still here, *she is living this moment and a life* and that is the main characteristic feature of a living thing.

The manner in which the shadows are formed here is just like a MUSIC which can be seen and it is such an amazing thing.

Feeling of anxiety about the idea of the proportions and ratio is absolutely normal for the beginners.

Don't limit yourself into practicing only few number of poses. Practice over long time period gets you enough experience to let you gain sense of proportions.

Always remember key steps-
- Use of lines
- Development of form
- Simplified anatomical design
-

The nipple is never in the center of the breast. It is located slightly down and outwards. Breast should be high but not too high.

To understand body structure and form you need to follow-
- Regular drawing
- Repeated practice

Body is not a complex form

Body is simple structure formed from jointed parts to jointed parts.

You don't have to be a fast learner to achieve big success

Just understand the fundamentals to become more confident.

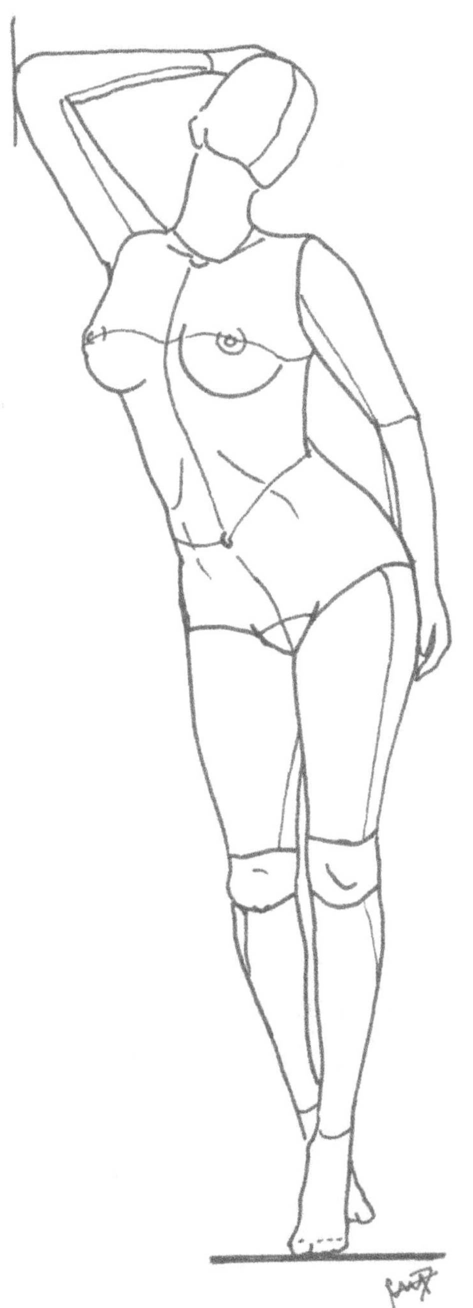

One unique thing about standing position is in order to create balance for body when entire weight is transferred on the legs, there is a locking of knee joint.

When *legs locks at knee joint at a certain position, it gives stability to the stance* and proper body weight distribution.

Knee is pushed back when the legs gets locked

On your left you can notice the prominence of the waist.

Human body is made up of lots of parts working together forming a structure .

If you keenly observe the body does appear in wave form and looks like "S" alphabet shape here.

Parts forming the profile of this simple figure

- Head and shoulder
- Neck
- Chest out
- Stomach in
- Right arm behind the back
- Left arm on which the body leans on
- Heels together
- Joints connecting part by part

Now look at the figure as a whole

- The proportion
- The view
- The pose
- The gesture
- The structure
- The construction

Combine all the above components and you realize that drawing a human figure is ain't as complicated as it sounds. Once you get the elements of figure right, 90% of the job is done

Here also look at the way the body is tilted at angle to the ground.

The body is leaning on a support of a chair.

The weight of the body is evenly distributed between the chair and the legs, balancing the center of gravity using two supports.

Try to communicate the natural design of the figure.

Notice how the spine is responsible for balancing the body.

The body taken the support of one leg and other leg is hanging free.

Spine is connecting bridge between the leg and the arm.

Notice how the arms are supporting the upper body and maintaining the balance.

Legs are always variety in shape but generally larger the buttocks, thicker the thighs.

Backside view of a standing female always stresses about the curves of female as shown above. There are plenty of different configuration in creation of different poses. Regardless types of pose, always build up the sketch in stages.

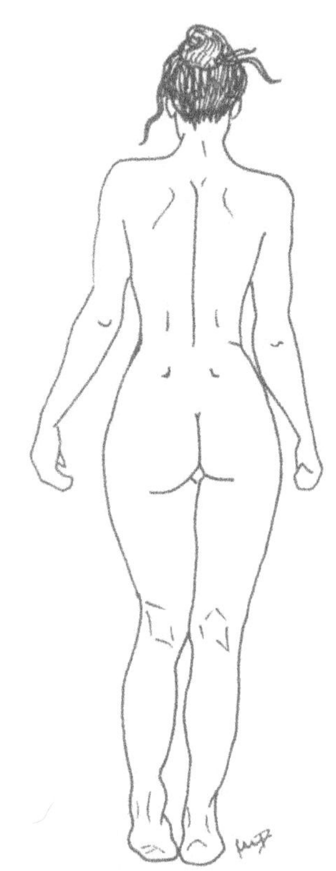

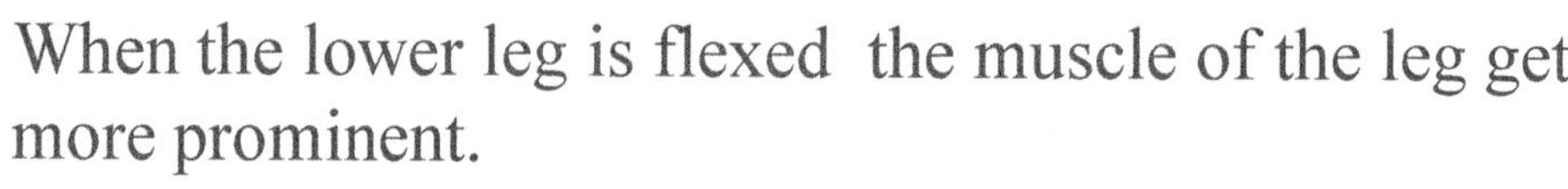

When the lower leg is flexed the muscle of the leg get more prominent.

Patella and both the condyles become more evident.

Back surface of thigh is found between lower part of buttocks and calf.

Muscles of legs appear prominent when the leg is flexed or extended at the knee joint.

Female Figure in sitting

It is easy to stick onto the eight head unit proportion when it comes to model in standing position. Now lets work on how to sketch something in other than standing position which deviates from this standard eight unit proportion.

Seated figure ends up measuring six head unit because of bending at head, hips and knees which reduces overall height

Weight of the body rests on the hips, elbows and foot when in seated position.

Most people say one cannot draw figures without the knowledge of anatomy, but that is a misunderstanding.

All the artists from before have done several masterpieces without great deal of anatomical knowledge.

Beginners have the tendency to copy Master's work. Instead explore your own ways, make mistakes, get criticized and learn in the process. Draw using which ever method that suits you.

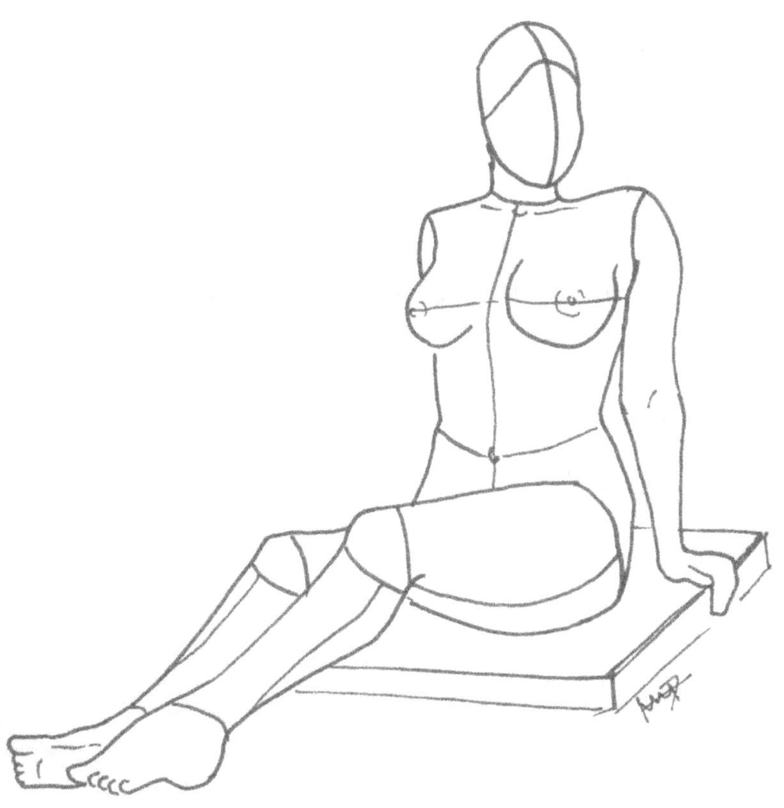

The position and the view point of this model is eye catching.

Position—sitting
View point— sideway view

The way the weight of the body is supported is mesmerizing.

Turning and twisting of torso and the head towards back is causing the folds on the neck and the flanks.

The way the buttress rests on the chair with support of those legs gives that classy look here.

Draw what you can see, if you can draw correctly, your drawing will be all correct.

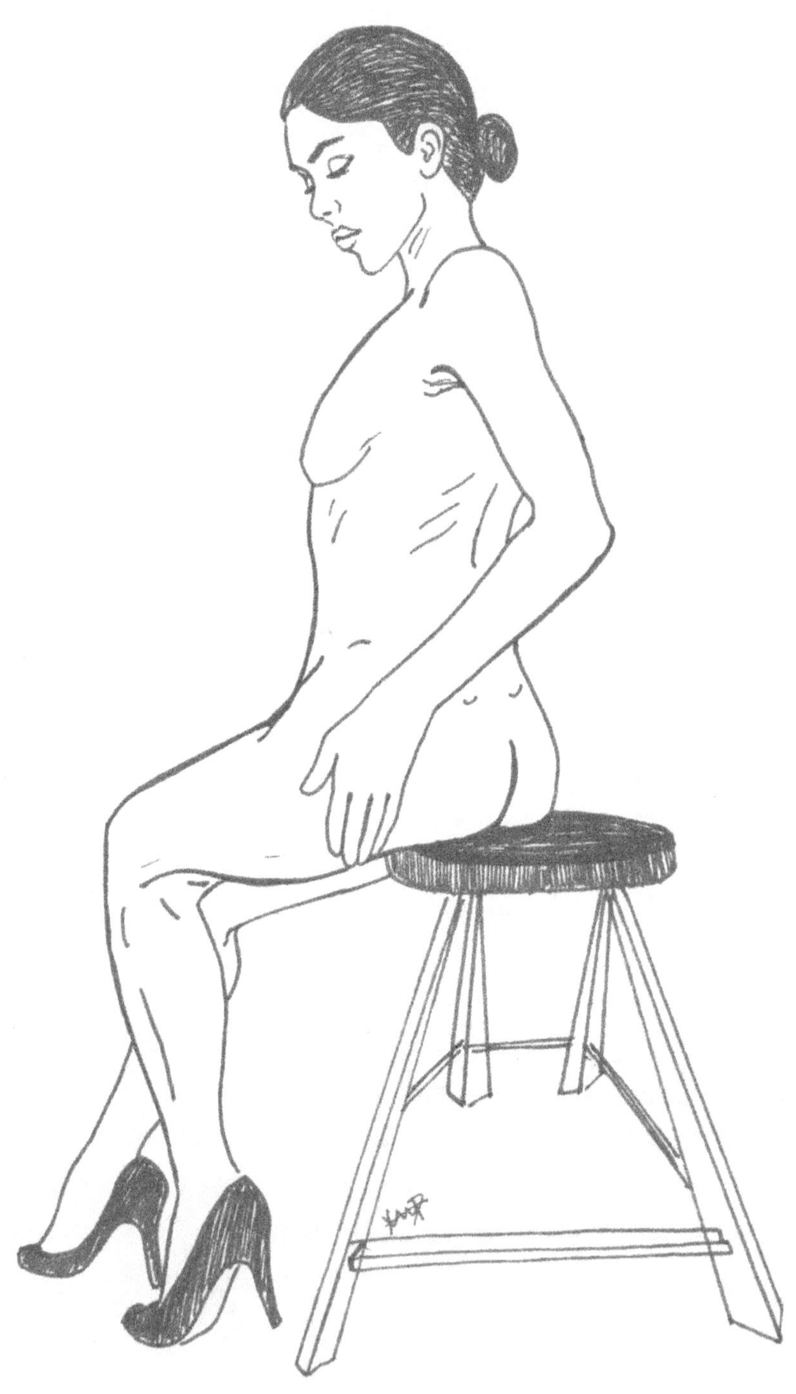

Look at how carefully I have shown the outline of this figure which is seated comfortably relaxed on the chair.

As an absolute beginner when you see model, its completely fine to start drawing by seeing only the outline.

Realizing how relaxed and comfortable the model is seated on the chair is very important, that's the gesture of the model which you are trying to figure out.

Look out for-
- *The way arms rest upon the armrest of the chair*
- *The way body is seated*
- *The way the breasts flatten out on the chest wall*
- *The way legs are dropped on the ground.*

Never see a figure merely for its shape, understands the emotions expressed by her.

Here the figure occupies good amount of space on a sheet of paper, its lines must be carefully looked upon in relation to the border lines.

Look at how the arms rests upon and how the body takes its shape in relation to the arm to attain a pose for maintaining balance.

When you sit and look at the model for the first time with a pencil in your hand, clear your mind all those preconceived ideas and thoughts. Such things should be eliminated, just draw what you see.

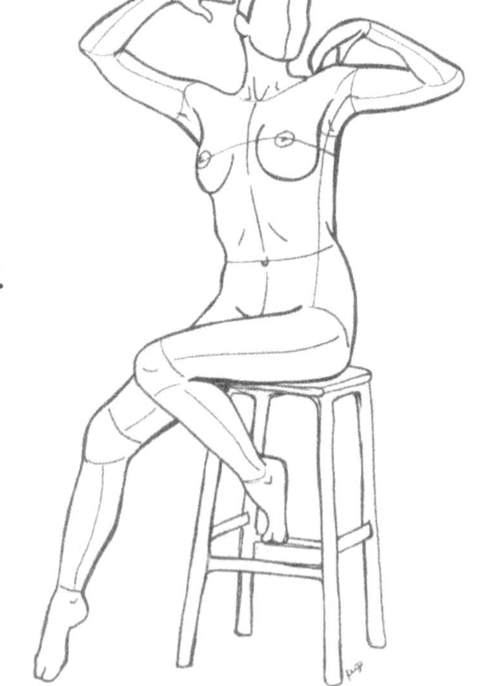

Here the figure is seated with arms folded up in the air, body stretched upwards and one leg falling on the ground while the other rests on the foot rest of the chair.

Try to feel what the model is expressing and just draw whatever your intuition guides you towards.

As explained earlier, look at the many shapes which forms the whole figure inside your head, put it on the paper.

It is extremely easy to get lost in the maze of detailing the figure and forgetting to work on the basics.

The blocks or the masses of body are levers moved by muscles.

Great deal of anatomical knowledge, sometimes can be more damaging than helpful.

Notice how the tension and compression of various poses affect the shape and structure of the body.

This is sort of pose that model can hold for 10-15 minutes. So be quick and try to memorize it and draw it from your memory later.

This posture is elegant and easy to draw. Just don't get carried away with the fine details.

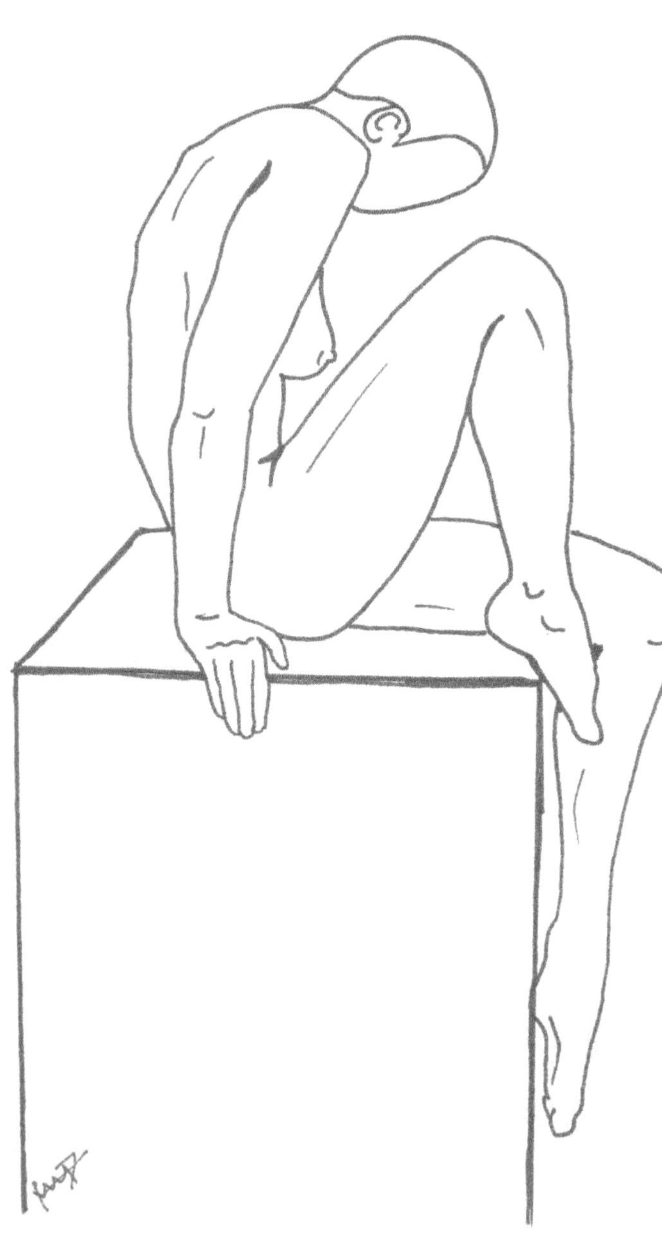

In this sitting position
1. Body tends to be in a relaxed position
2. The spine usually wont be erect as in standing position
3. Spine will be slightly bent
4. Legs fall downward and they tend to be relaxed
5. Arms tend to support the body posture
6. Head is usually flexed

Using the midline is the key aspect to align upper body in proper position especially when body is in seated position.

Basic steps
- Start with loose gesture sketch
- Refine drawing
- Add more details
- Ink image using artistic pens

It is essential that you draw everyday.

Repeated drawing of human figure will enable you to gain a visual understanding of body form and structure.

Look at importance of—
- *Twisting*
- *Turning*
- *Bending*
- *Anatomy*

Notice how cylindrical forms are being represented here, the legs are mostly cylindrical form.

Here, this front view shows how to handle areas of intersection by thinking of the figure. It is simplified sketch of distribution of body weight and balance.

Drawing shows figure in sitting position and figure holding all the weight on the left side. The pelvis is raised on the right side and dropped on the left side.

On the right side area of the bone have moved away from each other, area in between is pulled and shows a stretch.

Initially give 2-3 minutes for gesture drawing that focuses on placing the land-mark perfectly.

Feel that action in her arms, shoulders and her presence.

Natural attitude of the head depends on the curve of the body and the posture the models gets into.

The sitting pose though simple as it may seem to look at, each part of models body gets affected due to the stretching and relaxation of the body parts simultaneously.

On evaluation, see the contraction in the abdominal muscles or stretching of the muscles of the arms and compression, overlapping in the legs.

Head tilt will also give the direction in which the model is facing towards.

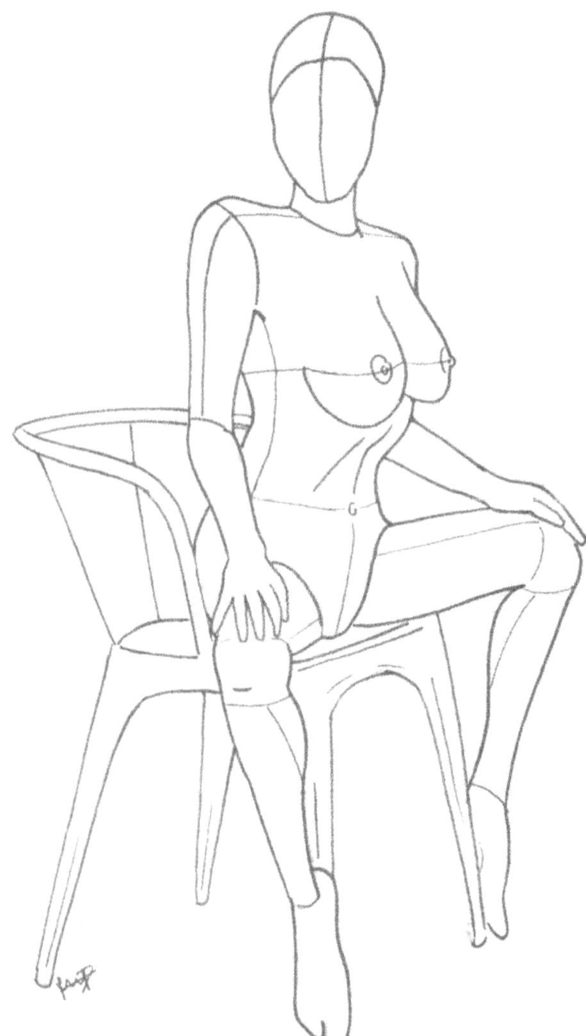

The midline from the head passing below i.e., **Central axis of the torso** *is the line of action.*

Other lines over arms and the legs indicate the rhythmic movement of the figure

It gives flow to the structure, interconnects various components and unifies the figure, giving a sense of movement even though the figure is still as standing water.

Don't forget that the developing in constructive drawing is not necessarily the desired finished product.

Develop methods to display unseen part, as in here where the model's right hand which we can't see resting on her chest and left shoulder.

Here the muscles of the back extends out into the arms.

There is a voluntary effort to hold the body in this posture.

Hips and knees are flexed while the foot is extended at the ankle.

Also the body appears as sort of a geographical terrain.

Shoulder joint bones appears prominent here along with those knuckles on the dorsal aspect of the hand.

Just because everyone has the same basic anatomy, doesn't mean it fits exactly the same on that model you draw.

Don't let your ideas blind you to the character of a specific pose.

As you can see here her locked arms are supporting torso and pushing shoulders up and forwards. Raised legs is causing folds on belly.

Sketching the body shapes according to the body of the reference model is always easy.

Unlike the portrait drawing where in you need to have pin point precision to make it look like same person, it is ok in case of figure drawing because few things are overlooked by the normal eyes.

Notice how firm the model is seated here.

Thighs are soft and heavy due to presence of fat and with knee being flexed the mass of legs appear more prominent.

Most of the upper body is covered and lies hidden behind the legs.

Head and lower body with arms appear prominent in this sitting posture.

Notice how prominent the clavicle bones appear.

Digits of the hands and legs that is the fingers and the toes are key aspect . Work on it properly

Female Figure in sleeping

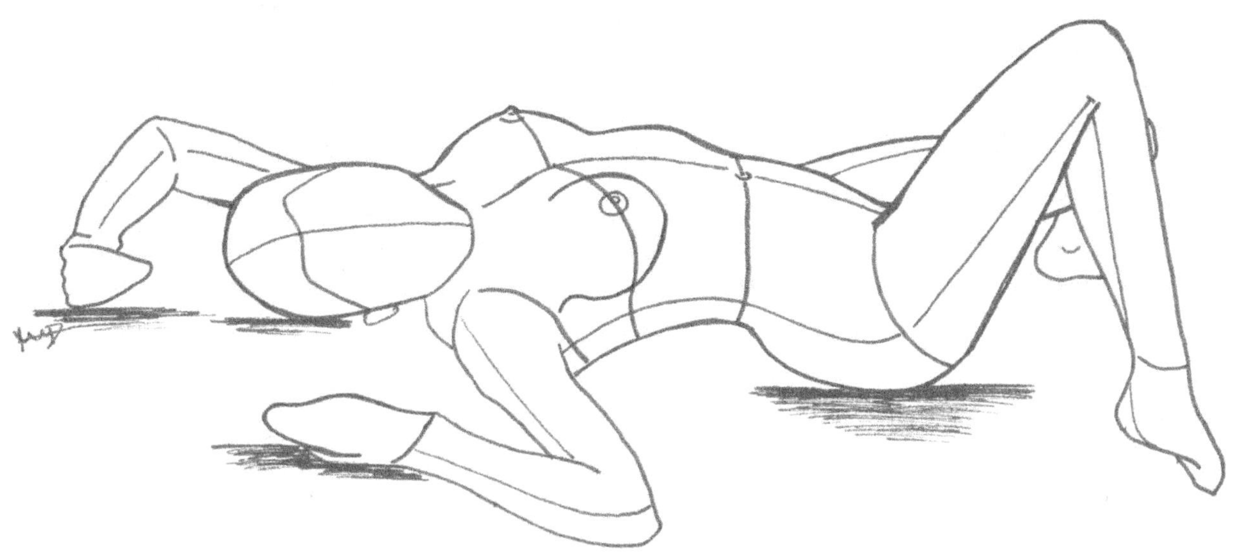

Upright figure is more familiar to eye compared to the one in sleeping position because we normally see people in standing and sitting pose more than in sleeping pose.

Weight falls on the back and head and dependent parts of the body

Measuring proportion becomes bit tricky in this scenario

There will be series of overlapping body parts making it difficult to draw.

The below picture is a complex form of sleeping posture with a high arched back and twisting of the body.

- There is a prominent rib cage with it

- The legs raised makes thighs become prominent

- The outstretched arms makes armpit appear deep

- The stomach flattens out

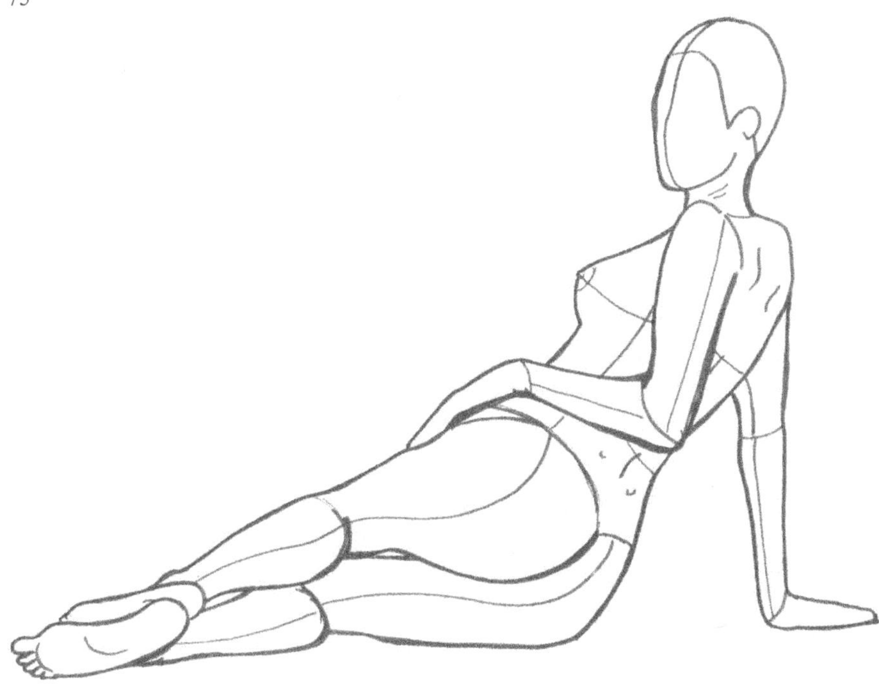

Body is twisted here in such a way that the hips is the presenting prominent part and is at a different angle to that of the shoulder.

Weight gets distributed over the right leg and the right arm.

Try to look for the hidden construction of the form.

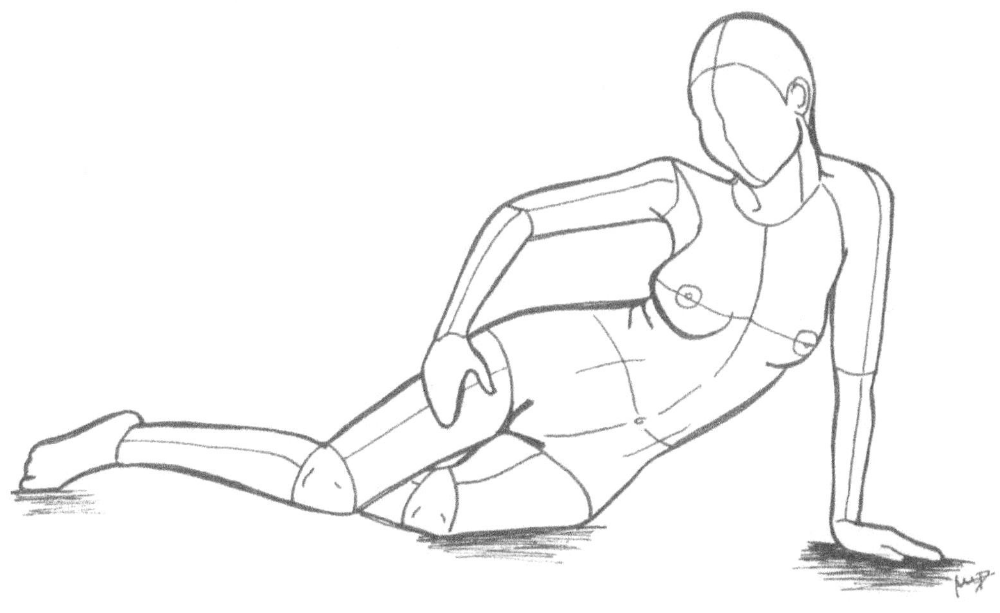

This drawing is a thorough drawing where focus is just upon getting the proportions right.

Model character is simple with resting posture

Also look at how oddly the right arm rests over the thighs.

Female Figure on couch

Models are most relaxed when they rest on the couch. Weight usually is transferred to one side of the body in such posture.

Make sure you include good amount of details about couch too.

Just focus on inter-relation of each parts, how both legs rest in relation to each other, how arms takes its shape, how head is in relation to the neck.

Female Figure in kneeling

Usually the kneeling figure appears six head units tall.

Kneeling posture is expressive and bit dynamic.

The weight of the body usually falls on the knees, one or both knees, sometimes also on elbow and hands.

With model taking this pose, the rib cage appears too prominent with expressive thighs and calves.

Feet is always a bit tricky.

To sketch feet, try to see the feet as simple shapes. Begin with the big toe and clump the small toes as one unit.

Look at the direction of the flow of lines from the head to toes.

Look at the non-parallelism of those lines making sure the form appears three dimensional.

We are adding extra appeal to the figure to ourselves, *the effective learning of this three dimensional flow of lines can do miracles* to us when once we have learned it.

The model appears here in a peculiar way such that there is a thrust on the upper body being pushed forwards simultaneously having upward pull by the arms.

Notice the flow of lines along different plane demonstrating three dimensional form.

The curve of the line from the nipple along the breast to the axilla indicates volume of the breasts.

The curve of the line on the thighs flowing down to the ankles indicates volume and bulk of the thighs.

Overall the picture should appear as a whole once you are done finishing the sketch.

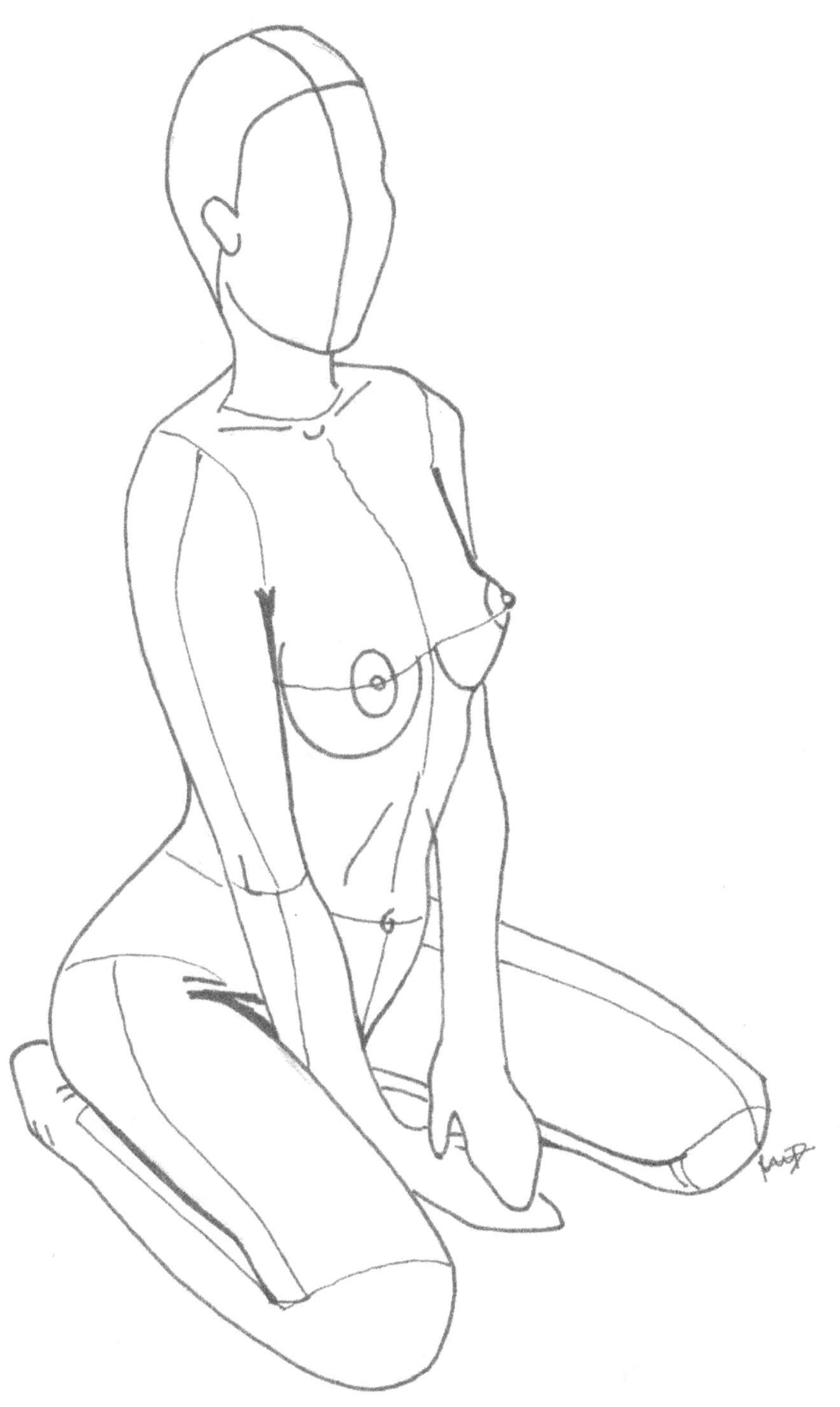

Drawing undergoes constant changes as you are in the process of creating it.

Always remember the initial step is to fix the important contours, the lines that best capture the movements of the figure

As you work over drawing figures over and over again, you start to gain confidence in your ability to represent the human figure in an exact manner.

Here the view is unique, you are trying to see the model in such a way that it lies below your eye level.

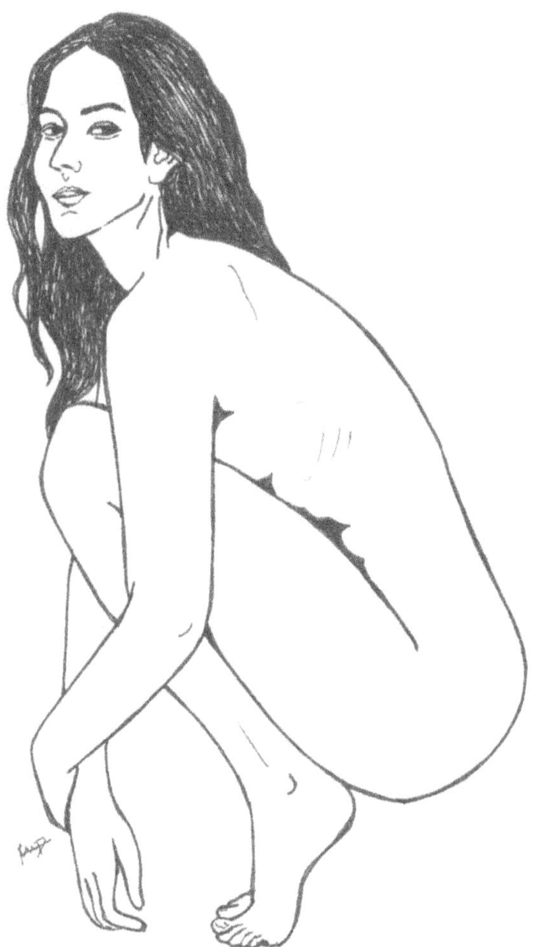

This has mainly one key aspect of how analyzing the body maintaining its balance in pose like this.

Unseen balance is maintained by the arm and seen balance is maintained by the toes demonstrating how fabulously the human body works.

Torso twisted here on the pelvis and the head tilted on the neck here in oblique fashion.

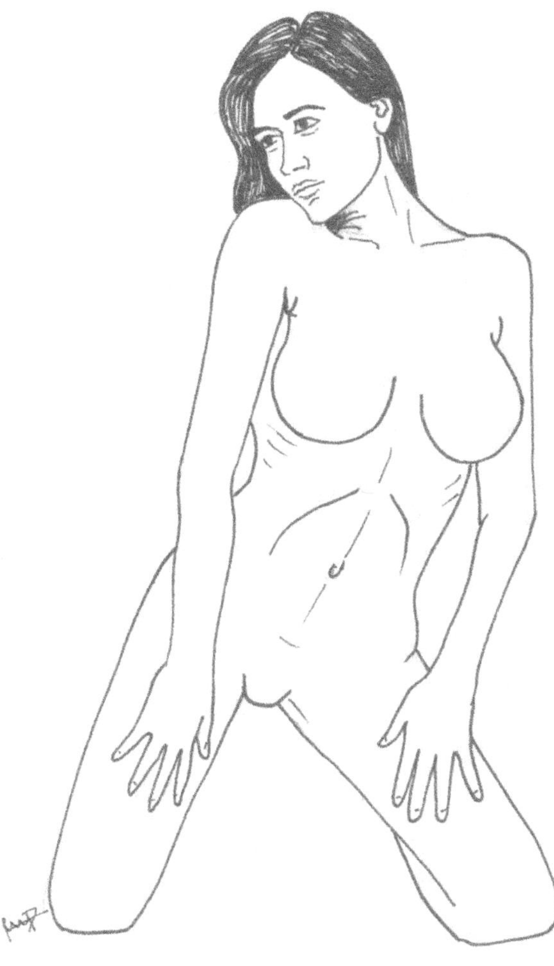

Here the model is perfectly balanced on the both knees.

Head is tilted on one side. The stretch of head makes a pull over abdomen creating folds.

The prominence of the shoulder is very clearly noted here.

Folds on the right side of the neck indicated the turning of head toward that side.

I've used descriptive lines whose primary goal is to describe the profile and the volume.

Even though the figure drawing on the left may seem to be complex, when you look at the breakdown of the sketch you do realize that its just composition of most basic simple forms.

It totally is your part to arrange these basic forms and place them in spots matching the characteristic feature of the model.

Here is a pose where the model is completely bowing down to ground in kneeling position

The arch of the back is very prominent with spine curved and bent to its maximum capacity

The weight of the body is thrown forward onto the head, legs and arms.

Drawing is a definitive logical process. Logic says stick to the basics and draw as simple as possible.

When you study the model the way I've demonstrated here notice that the-
- The head is way too extended here.

- The neck is stretched and the torso is pulled upwards.

- The thighs, hips and legs are just resting and not playing that significant role here.

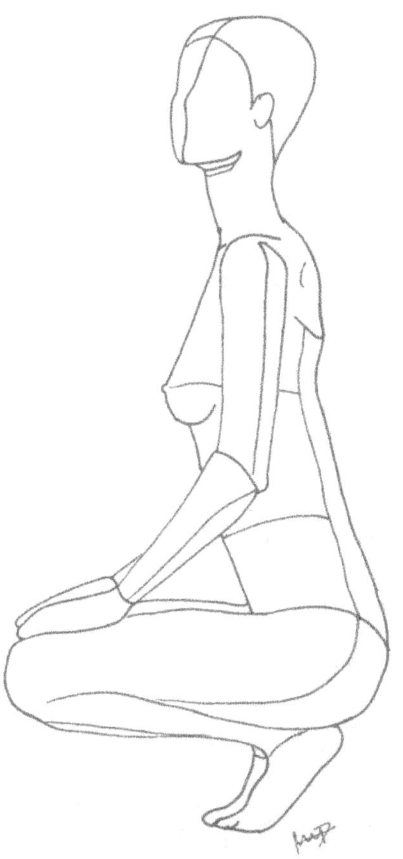

Lets go through this demonstration here-
- The angle used for the neck, shoulder, hips and the back is the same
- Knee and hand are aligned to each other and are equally playing important role in balancing the body.
- Weight is supported by the foot and the ankle

Let's look at plan of approach for this sketch.
1. Observation
2. Putting knowledge into work
3. Forming basic element
4. Interconnecting the elements
5. Forming final outline
6. Carrying it through to the completion

Work space: You can practice in space given below to draw which you have learned till now & see how much you've improved from before

Also read….
Portrait drawing made easy for beginners - detailed step by step art tutorial book by Dr. Manjunath V Rao
Available across various online platform including Amazon and flipkart.